Any of us who have f(
faith and doubt" or su
to make of biblical cla
a hospitable invitation to take a long second look. Maybe even to
venture through the doors of a church. Jared Ayers meets readers
in the shadowy places of uncertainty not with arguments but with
stories that help even the deeply disenchanted reimagine a life in
which faith is sustaining and a vigorous community of thoughtful
believers is possible.

> **Marilyn McEntyre,** speaker, professor, and author of numerous books, including *Caring for Words in a Culture of Lies, Word by Word, Dear Doctor,* and more

Jared's book is a compelling look at how Christians engage wisely
and winsomely in this cultural moment. Jared's exceptional writing,
engaging storytelling, and deep experience as a pastor and church
planter offer connection and credibility to readers. I'm very excited
to promote this book as it's being birthed into the world.

> **Chuck DeGroat,** professor of pastoral care and Christian spirituality at Western Theological Seminary and author of *When Narcissism Comes to Church, Toughest People to Love, Wholeheartedness,* and more

In an age of disillusionment and disenchantment, we need wise
pastoral voices who bring a curious mind, an awakened heart, and
a lively, compassionate pen to our many perplexing questions. We
need voices like Jared Ayers's, and I'm excited to support the work
he's creating and the beautiful gospel it evokes.

> **Winn Collier,** director of the Eugene Peterson Center for Christian Imagination at Western Theological Seminary and author of *A Burning in My Bones; Love Big, Be Well;* and more

Jared Ayers says this is a book for those on the borderlands of faith. He is qualified to say this because (1) he wrote it and (2) he has spent an enormous amount of time with people there and knows what he's talking about. But as I read, I kept thinking, *This is a book for the church.* Jared knows the gospel. Knows the beauty and power of what has been entrusted to a community of faith. And in an age of disillusionment with and confusion about what the gospel actually is, Jared, a sage, scholar, and warmhearted pastor, is giving it to us all over again—pressed down, shaken together, and running over. This is a book for both the church and those at the borderlands. A book to be savored.

Andrew Arndt, author of *A Strange and Gracious Light* and more

Who knew that a book of theology could be written with such wit and wisdom? Who knew that a book of pastoral ministry could brim with thoughtful, perceptive, and wise insights? This book is both. The combination of theology and pastoral wisdom here is compelling in our present context of deep anxiety and confusion. Jared Ayers offers a fresh telling of the Christian story and connects it at every turn with real people's real lives. It is a book for people who believe, who doubt, who question, and who yearn.

Leanne Van Dyk, president emerita of Columbia Theological Seminary

Clear, compelling, and propelled by a soaring Christology, Jared Ayers breathes fresh air into the fathomless mystery of what it means to have a wounded healer God on our side. For a doubting, cynical generation, this pastoral, humble, persuasive voice is a giant step forward in the journey of faith seeking understanding.

Eric E. Peterson, founding pastor of Colbert Presbyterian Church

YOU CAN TRUST A GOD WITH SCARS

FAITH (AND DOUBT) FOR THE SEARCHING SOUL

JARED AYERS

Published in alliance with Tyndale House Publishers

NavPress.com

You Can Trust a God with Scars: Faith (and Doubt) for the Searching Soul

Copyright © 2025 by Jared Ayers. All rights reserved.

A NavPress resource published in alliance with Tyndale House Publishers

NavPress is a registered trademark of NavPress, The Navigators, Colorado Springs, CO. The NavPress logo is a trademark of NavPress, The Navigators, Colorado Springs, CO. *Tyndale* is a registered trademark of Tyndale House Ministries. Absence of ® in connection with marks of NavPress or other parties does not indicate an absence of registration of those marks.

The Team:
David Zimmerman, Publisher; Deborah Sáenz, Editor; Elizabeth Schroll, Copyeditor; Lacie Phillips, Production Assistant; Ron C. Kaufmann, Cover Designer; Cathy Miller, Interior Designer; Sarah Ocenasek, Proofreading Coordinator

Cover and interior photograph of paper texture copyright © by Mykhail Yenin/Depositphotos. All rights reserved.

Author photograph provided by author; used with permission. All rights reserved.

Unless otherwise indicated, all Scripture quotations are taken from the New Revised Standard Version Bible, copyright © 1989 National Council of the Churches of Christ in the United States of America. Used by permission. All rights reserved worldwide. Scripture quotation marked KJV is taken from the *Holy Bible*, King James Version. Scripture quotations marked MSG are taken from *The Message*, copyright © 1993, 2002, 2018 by Eugene H. Peterson. Used by permission of NavPress. All rights reserved. Represented by Tyndale House Publishers. Scripture quotations marked NIV are taken from the Holy Bible, *New International Version*,® *NIV*.® Copyright © 1973, 1978, 1984, 2011 by Biblica, Inc.® Used by permission. All rights reserved worldwide.

Some of the anecdotal illustrations in this book are true to life and are included with the permission of the persons involved. All other illustrations are composites of real situations, and any resemblance to people living or dead is purely coincidental.

For information about special discounts for bulk purchases, please contact Tyndale House Publishers at csresponse@tyndale.com, or call 1-855-277-9400.

ISBN 978-1-64158-996-3

Printed in the United States of America

31	30	29	28	27	26	25
7	6	5	4	3	2	1

To Monica, my Beatrice

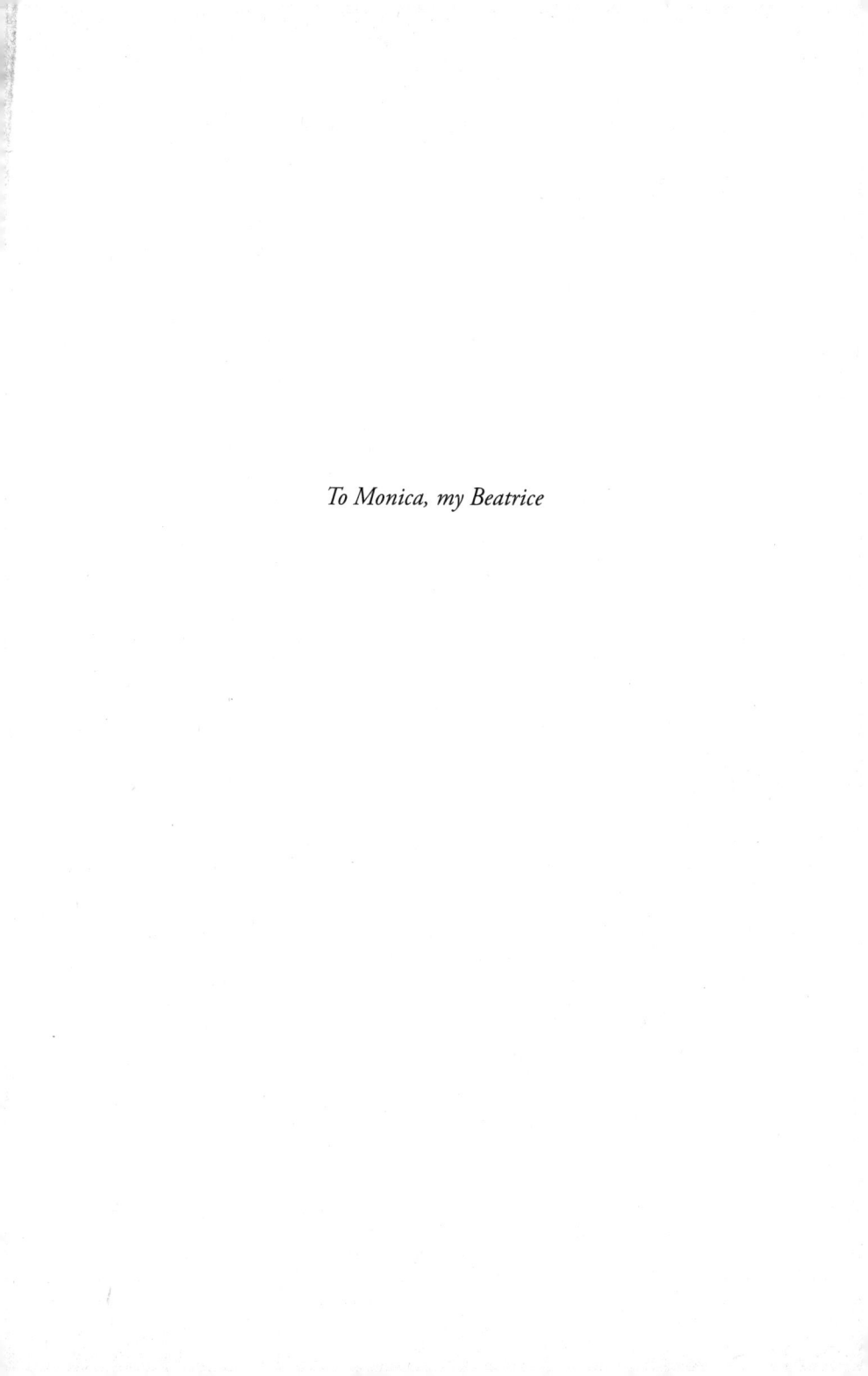

CONTENTS

INTRODUCTION For Those Who Fret about It *1*

CHAPTER ONE Heima
Our Longing for Home **13**

CHAPTER TWO Currents
The Conditions We're Swimming In **29**

CHAPTER THREE YHWH
Discovering God **43**

CHAPTER FOUR Miserable Offenders
Our Mutual Predicament **67**

CHAPTER FIVE God Incarno
What If God Were One of Us? **85**

CHAPTER SIX A Crucifix in a Bar
Why the Cross Is Good News **99**

CHAPTER SEVEN Nothing to Be Frightened Of
The Hope of Resurrection **115**

CHAPTER EIGHT I'll Be There in Spirit
Experiencing God's Spirit **129**

CHAPTER NINE She's a Harlot, She's My Mother
Why Bother with the Church? **139**

CHAPTER TEN Durable Welfare
Hope for Tomorrow, Hope for Today **155**

EPILOGUE Not Lying Anymore **167**
Acknowledgments **171**
Notes **173**

INTRODUCTION
For Those Who Fret about It

For a guy who sees no point in existence, you sure fret about it an awful lot.
Marty Hart in **TRUE DETECTIVE**

*Late have I loved you, Beauty so ancient and so new,
late have I loved you!
Lo, you were within,
but I outside, seeking there for you,
and upon the shapely things you have made I rushed headlong,
I, misshapen.
You were with me, but I was not with you.*
AUGUSTINE, *The Confessions*

My wife, Monica, and I have very different tastes in film, television, and literature, and mine tends to be significantly darker than hers. One evening several years ago on summer vacation at the Jersey Shore, after tucking our children into bed, I suggested we give the award-winning crime-noir television series *True Detective* a watch together. She made it ten minutes or so before informing me that if I wanted to continue watching, I'd be doing so alone.

And I did.

I binge-watched the eight episodes of *True Detective*'s inaugural season over the next thirty-six hours or so. Set in Vermilion Parish, a backwater precinct in rural Louisiana, the show centers on the relationship of state homicide detectives Marty Hart (played by Woody Harrelson) and Rust Cohle (played by Matthew McConaughey). Cohle is both intelligent and deeply troubled and has just transferred to the area after working undercover in a narcotics unit in Texas. His philosophizing and haunting nihilism immediately grate on Marty Hart, a lifelong local whose uncritical adherence to Bible-belt Christianity papers over his midlife restlessness, gnawing appetites, and marital infidelity. Harrelson and McConaughey's chemistry creates complex characters who over the arc of the series bristle at, cross, and eventually embrace each other.

One of my favorite moments of the series unfolds as Cohle and Hart set out to solve the murder of a young prostitute. As they follow leads, they stop at an outdoor revival service. Standing aloof at the edge of the tent, Rust Cohle surveys the crowd, scowling, and says, "What do you think the average IQ of this group is?"

Marty is taken aback: "What do you know about these people?" To which Cohle, continuing to look around, deadpan, replies, "Just observation and deduction: I see a propensity for obesity, poverty, a yen for fairy tales. Folks putting what few bucks they do have in the little wicker baskets being passed around. I think it's safe to say that nobody here is going to be splitting the atom, Marty."

They continue to argue under their breath at the edge of the crowd, and Cohle presses: "What's it say about life that you've got to get together, tell yourself stories that violate every law of the universe, just to get through the **** day?"

They continue to argue, and before he walks away, Marty turns to Rust and remarks, "Well, I don't use ten-dollar words as much as you. But for a guy who sees no point in existence, you sure fret about it an awful lot."[1]

This is a book for those who see no point in existence.

This is a book for those who fret about it.

And this book is for everybody who does some of both.

For much of my pastoral life, I've conversed in living rooms, on park benches, and in bars and cafés with people wondering about the Christian faith, curious about what it would mean to become a Christian or struggling with whether they can stay one.

The questions we ask in the borderlands between faith and doubt are as old as humanity. And many of them are written right into the text of the Scriptures. Listen, for example, to the ancient prayers set at the center of the Bible, the Psalms. Christians believe that Scripture is the Word of the Lord, God's discourse to the world in Christ Jesus. But the Psalms, uniquely, are both Holy Scripture and human praying—God's Word to us, and our words to God.[2]

And these canonized prayers gather up the big questions we ask and bring them to honest expression.

There are the anguished prayers of those who wonder if God's forgotten them:

How long, O Lord, will You forget me always?
How long hide Your face from me?[3]

And there are invocations that name the cruel unfairness of life—how it is that the corrupt enjoy lives of ease while good people suffer?

> I envied the revelers,
>   I saw the wicked's well-being:
> "For they are free of the fetters of death,
>   and their body is healthy.
> Of the torment of man they have no part,
>   and they know not human afflictions."[4]

There's even the canonized cry of someone who feels forsaken by God entirely, who screams their supplication up at a silent sky and hears nothing in return:

> My God, my God, why have You forsaken me?
>   Far from my rescue are the words that I roar.
> My God, I call out by day and You do not answer,
>   by night—no stillness for me.[5]

It is this derelict outburst that Jesus himself prays, in fact, as he comes to his end on the cross: "My God, my God, why have you forsaken me?"[6] Jesus, whom we Christians believe to be the human embodiment of the God we pray to, prays this very outburst of honest anguish. In his life, the masses flocked to Jesus for answers; but at his crucifixion, Jesus died asking our questions.

Doubt and disbelief are there as well, from the earliest Easter beginnings of the Christian movement. In the Gospel accounts of the first Easter morning, a solemn parade of bleary-eyed mourners make their way to Jesus' tomb in the predawn blackness. In Luke's version, several women arrive at the tomb with burial spices and embalming ointments, intending simply to offer their Teacher the dignity in death he was stripped of in his cruel crucifixion. But they don't find what they expect (the body of Jesus), and they discover what they couldn't have expected: two angelic figures, dressed in dazzling light, making the astonishing announcement that becomes the heart of the Christian gospel: "He is not here, but has risen."[7]

The women run, breathless, back to the eleven disciples who form Jesus' inner circle and who will go on to comprise the leadership of the Christian church. And what is their first response to the Good News of Easter? "These words seemed to them an idle tale, and they did not believe them."[8] English translators are actually kinder to the disciples here than Luke himself is: In Greek, the language this part of the Bible was originally authored in, the word often translated in English as "idle tale" is *lēros*, which means something more like "BS." The disciples, who became the first believers in the risen Jesus, were first the first disbelievers in Jesus.

Several years ago, someone stirred up controversy on Yale University's campus by placing a cross on its grounds during Holy Week, replacing the Latin letters *INRI* traditionally found in Christian artwork (which mean "Jesus of Nazareth, King of the Jews") with the letters *ROFL* (slang shorthand for "rolling on the floor laughing"). The cross created the predictable controversies about culture wars and free speech, but when I read this story, I was struck by the irony that this was actually closer to the initial response of the first Christians themselves to the Christian gospel.

"Lēros."

"BS."

"Fake news."

"ROFL."

EVERYBODY KNEW SOMEBODY

The winding journey through the terrain between doubt and faith is a trek humanity has long taken. And yet, in the twenty-first century, increasing numbers of would-be Christians, former believers, and those disaffected by the Christian church become mired as well by their struggle over the deep harm inflicted by the Christian church herself.

Peter and Jim[9] were my landlords for a couple of years; they owned the first apartment Monica and I called home when we lived in Philadelphia. We quickly became friends, and over glasses of pinot noir around the circle of chairs they'd gather on the sidewalk in front of their row home on Philadelphia's sticky summer nights, I gradually began to learn their stories. Both Peter and Jim were vaguely spiritual, and both also had a deep aversion to Christian institutions. As I asked why, they went on to tell me about life growing up in Italian, Catholic neighborhoods in midcentury South Philly. "In those days," Peter told me, "priests abusing boys in the neighborhood was an open secret. Everybody knew somebody." Though they hadn't themselves suffered abuse, they'd watched schoolmates and neighbors be victimized by the church's leaders—and that had left lasting damage in their lives.

It's only in the last couple of decades that we've come to realize how widespread stories like Peter and Jim's really are. In 2002, a group of journalists at *The Boston Globe*, mostly Roman Catholic themselves, broke a story about Cardinal Bernard Law knowingly covering up clergy sexual abuse in his Boston parishes.[10] Their reporting wound up winning a Pulitzer Prize—and it also touched off what has become a reckoning for the

Roman Catholic Church in almost all of America's big cities and in parishes around the world.

And it's by no means only Roman Catholic Christians who bear the scars of harm done in and by the church. The Protestant church has its own ugly history with which to contend as well. The church in America has been complicit in chattel slavery, practiced and endorsed race-based segregation, and been party to its own share of physical, sexual, emotional, and spiritual abuses. In the last several years, headlines around the country have been filled with one high-profile Christian leader after another caught up in scandal and disgrace. As I write these words, yet another well-known pastor is currently making headlines for the way his church defended a teacher at their school who had been convicted of multiple accounts of abuse and the fact that they also excommunicated the man's wife for separating from her husband.[11] The widespread reality of this ugliness—the hypocrisy, dysfunction, and abuse often found in the church—make many feel as if they can no longer associate themselves with the Christian faith.

A CONVERSATION WITH MYSELF

Not only is this book a collection of conversations I've had with friends, neighbors, and congregants as they've migrated between faith and doubt, but it also encompasses internal dialogue from my own meandering journey.

Honest intellectual inquiry and back-and-forth dialogue with good friends who see the world very differently than I do has precipitated plenty of fretting.

What if my whole system of beliefs is mistaken?

What if I've built my whole life on an outdated fairy tale?

Twenty-odd years spent as a pastor has meant that I've collected more than a few scars from the ugliness of religious people too—the hypocrisy, manipulation, backbiting. After seeing headlines of yet another tragic case of abuse, after anguishing over yet another congregant whitewashing bigotry and racism in pious platitudes, after suffering a betrayal by a core church member whose wedding I'd performed, whose children I'd baptized, whose crises I'd showed up for on a moment's notice—well, after a couple of decades of all that, I've wondered whether the institution I serve hasn't lost the plot of the One whose Name we bear.

I've walked with enough suffering people that I've had to wonder, given how cruel life can be, and how seemingly random our hardships are, whether there's really a God worth believing in behind it all. I know what it's like to pray your heart out for someone and for those prayers to seemingly go nowhere. These questions aren't just ones I've fielded—they're ones I've lived.

That said, this book is an extended conversation about why, even given our own whispering doubts and the wreckage of church-inflicted pain we live with, I still think it's a good, true, beautiful thing to be a follower of Jesus. This conviction doesn't reside in me *despite* all the wonderings and struggles articulated here—it's there, and there more deeply, *because of* the honest, even painful, process of engaging them. So I'd love to converse with you in these pages about the Christian story, explore the doubts and struggles we have with it, and see if there isn't a way forward through the ambivalent spiritual territory many of us know all too well.

INTRODUCTION

BLACK & BREW

In our first years in Philadelphia, my family lived in a two-bedroom, five-hundred-square-foot Trinity-style brick row house tucked into a narrow side street in East Passyunk. Our dog, Baxter, and our toddler, Brennan, occupied one bedroom, which left Monica and me, our newborn son, Kuyper, and our church's "office"—my laptop, a home printer, and a few boxes of documents—to share the other room. Space was scarce to go over my sermon notes, so I'd begin many of my Sundays at a neighborhood café. In the stillness of Sunday's early hours, I'd slide out of bed and attempt to tiptoe my way down our creaking stairs and across our old oak floors without waking either of our kids. After escaping through the front door, I'd walk the tangle of narrow South Philly streets east and south to Black & Brew, which sat just a block up the street from the neighborhood square on Passyunk Avenue.

I'd enter as they'd open for the day at 6 a.m. and spread my notes, Bible, huevos rancheros, and Americano with cream across my usual table in the back of the café beneath the bay window. Most of those Sunday mornings, there were just three of us in Black & Brew as the sun rose and streamed across the dense, sleepy neighborhood: the woman working the early shift, barista and chef for the few customers who might wander in at that hour; me, nose buried in Bible, books, notes—and Daniel.

Daniel would usually sit at the bar, perched attentively over a plate of eggs Benedict and a cup of hot black coffee, scruffy beard tracing a slender jawline that just barely escaped the shadow of his herringbone flatcap. He was finishing his

Saturday night as I was starting my Sunday morning. On Saturday nights, Daniel would club his way up and down Thirteenth Street and the surrounding area, migrating from ICandy to L'Etage or Dirty Franks or the U Bar or sometimes a house party for drinks. When Saturday night was fully spent, he'd make a last stop at Black & Brew for some eggs before stumbling up his apartment steps next door to sleep through the morning hours.

The first few Sundays that Daniel and I spent occupying neighboring tables, we each kept our faces buried in breakfast and what was in front of us—sermon notes in my case, and whatever copy of the *New Yorker*, *Long Live Vinyl*, or *VICE* magazine that Black & Brew had left out for customers to peruse in his. But one Sunday, I had a vague sense of his gaze wandering again and again to settle on my turned back, Bible, and shuffle of papers. After finishing his breakfast, he deposited his cup and plate in the dish bin near the door, opened it to step out into the chilly morning air, and turned to me as he left, inquiring, "Is that, like, a Bible or something?"

I told him it was, introduced myself, and asked his name.

"Daniel." Then, after a short silence: "Are you some kind of priest or pastor?"

I nodded, admitted I was, and divulged that I was looking over my notes for our worship service that day.

"Wow. Really?! . . . Well, see you next Sunday, I guess, Father."

He breezed out the door. I listened to the thump of Daniel's ascent up the steps on the other side of the wall to his second-floor apartment to end his Saturday night. I felt sure I had scared him off—that next weekend he'd surely find somewhere else to enjoy his eggs and coffee in peace, somewhere that wouldn't put him in such dangerous proximity to a Christian minister.

But I was wrong. When I walked into Black & Brew the next Sunday morning, there he was: same seat at the bar, same eggs Benedict, hollandaise spilling over the side of the plate, same flatcap. We exchanged a knowing nod as I sat down, placed my order, and arranged the contents of my bag at my usual table. To my surprise, after a few minutes, I saw a shadow across my right shoulder and turned to discover Daniel standing at the edge of the table. "So what are you talking about this Sunday, Father?"

I don't remember the text I was preaching on or the topic of the sermon for that Sunday, but I do remember staring at Daniel, then staring down at my notes, then staring back at him again and having not the slightest idea what to say. I fumbled around and eventually got there, attempting to relate whatever selection from Exodus or Isaiah or John we would attend to that day. We talked for a few moments, and then Daniel left as usual, thump-thumping up the stairs next door.

This bit of sermon discussion happened this way, at that back table, most Sundays over the next few years: several sips of an Americano, a few bites of breakfast, and then, "Hey, Father, what are you talking about today?" It was the best preaching class in which I've ever enrolled. I'd taken courses to learn the Scriptures, courses to enable me to preach and teach them in the context of a church community, and courses to sharpen and hone my communication skills. But I had zero idea how to translate the gospel proclamations of these ancient texts for someone like Daniel—someone who knew almost nothing of the Christian story, whose cultural vocabulary didn't include the insider speak of my faith, and whose life and family experiences only sporadically included entering a church building. Those conversations with Daniel forced me to wrestle with questions I had never seriously considered about Jesus, the Bible, and God; they compelled me to relearn the language of faith in a way that would be meaningful and jargon-free for someone like Daniel; and they ultimately helped me find my voice in conversing about life, death, and the Father, Son, and Spirit to my many friends like Daniel who live their lives outside the decaying ruins of Christendom. Week by week, to this day, as I sit in my study with piles of books, that same Bible perched on a lectern, and scribbles of notes and ideas, prepping for the weekly work of preaching and teaching, I picture Daniel easing into the chair across from me to ask that same question: "What are you talking about today, Father?"

Think of what follows here as an extension of those conversations Daniel and I had Sunday by Sunday as we sat in Black & Brew. I'd love to include you in them. And I hope you'll pull up a chair and bring with you your questions and puzzles about faith, your cynicism and pain, and your flickering inklings of desire or hope or joy.

CHAPTER ONE

HEIMA

Our Longing for Home

Great are you, O Lord, and surpassingly worthy of praise. . . . You have made us for yourself, and our hearts are restless until they rest in you.

AUGUSTINE, *The Confessions*

Formed in the 1990s, by 2006 the Icelandic band Sigur Rós had achieved international critical acclaim and widespread commercial success. After finishing one of their world tours, they returned to Iceland to play a series of free, unannounced concerts in far-flung towns throughout their native country, which they filmed and released together as a documentary. In a deserted fishing town, a protest camp adjacent to a controversial dam, and an isolated highland wilderness, Sigur Rós performed their unique brand of elegant, symphonic post-rock. The soaring transcendence of their music matched the stark, rugged landscape of Iceland, which served as the backdrop for the film. Bassist and multi-instrumentalist Georg Hólm described the genesis of the project in an interview, saying, "I sometimes get this strange and sort of uncontrollable urge to want to go home."[1] The title of the film? *Heima*, which is Icelandic for both "at home" and "homeland."

HOMELAND

This ache for a homeland—for a heima from which we are dislocated in some way—is territory we all come to know sooner or later. It resides silently beneath all our successes and achievements, sneaks up on us in our quiet, wondering moments, convulses us in our lives' catastrophes.

As we'll come to see, the Christian story claims that this longing is woven into the very fabric of what it means to be human.[2] The author Frederick Buechner observes,

> No matter how much the world shatters us to pieces, we carry inside us a vision of wholeness that we sense is our true home and that beckons to us. It is part of what the book of Genesis means by saying that we are made in the image of God.[3]

This inescapable yearning for our "true home," as Buechner describes it, comes to gnaw at us all in different ways.

HOMESICK

For some, it surfaces as a nagging thirst for spiritual experience, a craving to connect to a Reality beyond what we can see, measure, or observe. This appetite stubbornly persists, even among the deeply secular. A feature piece in the *Atlantic* a few years ago chronicles this phenomenon; it acknowledges the widespread decline of participation in religious institutions among people in North America and Europe and the dramatic rise of self-identified "nones"—people who claim no association to any religious body. But the author, whose article is titled "Atheists Are Sometimes More Religious than Christians," notes how spiritual practices endure even among the growing numbers of the un- and disaffiliated. She chronicles the phenomenon of "atheist churches"; the "Beyoncé Mass" that a San Francisco cathedral held in 2018; and the Catholic-themed Met Gala of the same year, featuring A-list celebrities parading the red carpet in papal tiaras, halos, angel wings, and crucifixes.[4]

Maybe you've never ventured into an "atheist church" or attended a worship service featuring the musical catalog of Queen Bey or worn a papal tiara to a party. But in my experience, this inner ache sneaks up on even the most skeptical among us. It might, for you, have materialized that time when you were hiking the Portuguese coast and found yourself swept up in the violent beauty of the surf cascading relentlessly down on the rocky shoreline. Or when you sat with a cup of hot black coffee in a canoe on an Adirondack lake in the pregnant stillness just before dawn. Or when you wandered the worn, dense tangle of stone streets in an ancient city you'd never visited before. In these moments, you catch yourself thinking that all this staggering, burgeoning beauty can't—just can't—have issued from some meaningless cosmic accident.

Or maybe the ache slid in late one night as you sat at a long table. It was the third or fourth hour of the dinner you put together for some people from disparate dimensions of your life. The whole night had a choreography you didn't even really intend: the way old and new friends mixed and mingled over oysters, cheese, and antipasto; the way the tastes and textures of the branzino you'd roasted over charcoal, the vegetables from the neighborhood market, and the bottles of Verdejo you'd picked up all accompanied one another; the unhurried meander of conversation, laughter, stories. It was late, and dark, and the lights had all long since gone out in your neighbors' windows. But in the opaque nighttime, as you looked around the table, everything was good, and whole, and connected. And you wondered if there was something somehow hallowed about this table, this food, this gathering of people—as if this meal might be a taste of some greater Feast.

Or maybe it's in music that you make out the echo of Home. The War on Drugs are playing "Thinking of a Place," and something about the shimmering, lilting layers of guitars and the yearning in Adam Granduciel's weather-beaten voice breaks something open in you. Or you actually turn off your phone and laptop so that you can attend in an undivided way to the pop and hiss of Miles Davis's *Kind of Blue* on vinyl. And for just a minute or two, it seems like the music is connecting you with a More that you don't know how to describe exactly except that you know that the music said it, or perhaps it came through the music, in a way you can't quite express.

For some, the yearning for a homeland to which we haven't arrived materializes as a restlessness, a wandering dissatisfaction. You find yourself wondering if you would feel more settled, more content, if you lived in a different city. If you'd rest easy in life if you could just make partner, or land a gig at that rival start-up, or start your own organization. If you might come to be more, well, *at home* if your house were just a bit bigger, or if you lived in a different neighborhood, or if you were sending your kids to more highly rated schools.

Maybe you think you'd finally be satisfied with yourself if you could find a spouse.

Or if your spouse were only different from the way they are.

Or if you could have kids.

Or if your kids were different from the way they are.

This wanderlust for an unencumbered future and an open road was immortalized more than half a century ago in Jack Kerouac's iconic novel *On the Road*. This semiautobiographical book—a restless, freewheeling tale of hitchhiking and road trips, jazz, sexual misadventures, and drugs—became the defining work of the counterculture movement. It has since shaped decades of music, film, literature, and culture. It's become the hallmark picture of what it means to belong to the Beat Generation. And yet, fascinatingly, Kerouac's writing was originally inspired by John Bunyan's *The Pilgrim's Progress*, a classic depiction of spiritual pilgrimage in which Christian, Bunyan's protagonist, goes searching for "an inheritance, incorruptible, undefiled, and that fadeth not away."[5] In fact, Kerouac, in defining what it meant to be "Beat," drew together the expression of exhaustion—"I'm beat!"—and the vision of the beatific—the "visio beatifica," or "vision of God."[6] In Christian theology, this phrase depicts the blissful, unhindered vision of God's glory that is the ultimate destiny of God's rescued people. Our wanderlust, the allure of the open road, of the new city: If we can see it, these are all signposts pointing toward Home.

IS EVERYTHING PERMITTED?

For others, this yearning begins to take shape as we puzzle over the passions that drive us and how they cohere (or don't) within the story of the world we inhabit. I'll never forget sitting with my friend Aaron several years ago as he wrestled with this. He had recently begun attending my church's worship services, and over a pint around the corner table at our neighborhood pub, he told me a bit of his story. Aaron was a young doctor from a wealthy family, and he had gone into medicine because he had a passion to provide healing to people in need. Rather than aim for a lucrative future in private practice in a wealthy suburb, as most of his peers from medical school had, Aaron had accepted an assignment in an under-resourced hospital in an impoverished and dangerous urban neighborhood.

"I've had this deep desire to help people for as long as I can remember," he told me. "But I'm also an atheist, so my beliefs tell me it doesn't matter if I live a life that helps other people or just myself. Living unselfishly doesn't matter in any ultimate way if life doesn't have any purpose."

While his gaze drifted out the window, after a silent minute, Aaron added, "I don't know what to do with that."

Neither do many of us. And neither did Albert Camus. Camus was a twentieth-century French existentialist philosopher and author. He came to believe that life was characterized by "the absurd": that absent religious beliefs to prop up our sense of meaning and significance, life is incomprehensible and meaningless. For Camus, inevitable death undermined the value of anything that preceded it in life. Paradoxically, he lived with a deep "moral fervour and intellectual intensity."[7] Camus called this his "revolt."[8] He insisted that the best way to respond to the supposed meaninglessness of existence is to treat it with the contempt of acting as if every aspect of human life really does matter in a final sense.

He wrote this quandary right into one of his signature novels, *The Plague*. In the early, solitary days of the COVID-19 quarantine, I picked up a copy of Camus's quintessential existentialist novel as we were in the first months of learning to weather our own plague. It's set in the French-Algerian city of Oran and follows Dr. Bernard Rieux as he responds to a growing plague in his city. At the beginning of the book, rats start vacating sewers and cellars and dying in the streets. Then a few people fall violently ill and die. Then the number of cases keeps multiplying. As disease sweeps through the city, Rieux comes to befriend Jean Tarrou, a noble character who happened to be in Oran at the plague's outbreak and who works with Rieux to organize teams of volunteers to combat the spread of disease.

In a moving moment, Rieux and Tarrou sit together on a roof one evening, after an exhausting day tending to the ailing. As they look out over the terraced rooftops of Oran's skyline and out to the sea beyond, Tarrou tells his story to Rieux, including how he'd come to care deeply about taking "the path of sympathy" toward others in life. And then, as the two talk, Tarrou continues:

> "It comes to this," Tarrou said almost casually, "what interests me is learning how to become a saint."
> "But you don't believe in God."
> "Exactly! Can one be a saint without God?—that's the problem, in fact the only problem, I'm up against today."[9]

Tarrou, tragically, becomes one of the last victims of the plague in Oran. Camus depicts Tarrou's death (in congruence with his life) heroically, befitting of an atheist who has become a saint. Tarrou's puzzle is the same one Aaron was wrestling with as he sat across the pub table from me. It's not that Christians, or adherents of other religions, are more moral than others. And it's not that secular people don't care about universal human rights or educational inequality or providing the world's poor with basic medical aid.

On the contrary, the world is filled with many, many people devoted to healing bodies and minds, to providing food and clean water to impoverished communities that lack access to them, to emancipating trafficked boys and girls, and more. This is the dilemma: Why? Someone who believes that life is absurd and meaningless and yet pursues "the path of sympathy" toward others—who gives their money generously or teaches underprivileged children or provides medical care to a Majority World village—chooses to live in a way at odds with their own beliefs about life.

Fyodor Dostoevsky sums up the related predicament of our mutual moral obligations in his *The Brothers Karamazov*. In a moment in which Dmitri Karamazov is in an argument with his brother Alyosha, he points out to his brother, "Without God and the future life? It means everything is permitted now, one can do anything. Didn't you know?"[10] Without God, you may choose to care that the poor have access to medical help or you may choose to believe that trafficking humans is evil or that ethnic cleansing is deplorable. But in the last analysis, you can't believe that all people must also believe those same things. Everything is permitted.

DANTE

Maybe this ache for heima hasn't been as abstract as all that for you. Perhaps it arrives in a more personal, visceral way. It could be that it collides with you at some juncture in life in which your whole existence seems like it's on some pointless, unwanted detour, and you're just lost. Your career has fallen apart, and you have no idea what you're going to do with yourself. The phone rings one afternoon with the test results that shatter your whole world. The person who said "I do" to you one day decides that they don't anymore, and now you're alone again.

In the summer of 2019, I took a sabbatical from pastoral work, and our family spent some time in Italy. I was exhausted: The prior couple of years had been wracked with crises, budgetary troubles, conflict. We were going to be in Florence for a bit, and I figured there couldn't be a better place to try reading Dante's famous *Divine Comedy* than in his hometown, so I stuffed a copy in my backpack before we left. The train we rode throttled down the track along the coast, from Cinque Terre south and east toward Florence. As the passenger seated next to me nodded off, I opened *The Divine Comedy* and read,

> *When I had journeyed half of our life's way,*
> *I found myself within a shadowed forest,*
> *for I had lost the path that does not stray.*
> *Ah, it is hard to speak of what it was,*
> *that savage forest, dense and difficult,*
> *which even in recall renews my fear:*
> *so bitter—death is hardly more severe!*[11]

Those famous first lines of Dante's masterpiece were a mirror to me. Something in that moment crumbled inside me, and the pages were soon stained wet with the hot tears that just wouldn't stop coming. My life had become bitter, dense, difficult. I'd lost the path. I needed to get Home.

INCONSOLABLE SECRET

C. S. Lewis was a literature professor at Oxford University through the middle of the twentieth century. He lived much of his life as an atheist until, to his own surprise, he found himself convinced of the veracity and beauty of the Christian faith. In an important essay he wrote several years after his conversion, entitled "The Weight of Glory," he explores these incessant, unfulfilled desires for our homeland, which he calls "our own far-off country." These longings, which lie below the waterline of every human life, Lewis calls our "inconsolable secret":

> In speaking of this desire for our own far-off country, which we find in ourselves even now, I feel a certain shyness. I am almost committing an indecency. I am trying to rip open the inconsolable secret in each one of you—the secret which hurts so much that you take your revenge on it by calling it names like Nostalgia and Romanticism and Adolescence; the secret also which pierces with such sweetness that when, in very intimate conversation, the mention of it becomes imminent, we grow awkward and affect to laugh at ourselves; the secret we cannot hide and cannot tell, though we desire to do both. We cannot tell it because

it is a desire for something that has never actually
appeared in our experience. We cannot hide it because
our experience is constantly suggesting it, and we
betray ourselves like lovers at the mention of a name.
Our commonest expedient is to call it beauty and
behave as if that had settled the matter. . . . But all this
is a cheat.[12]

We have, each of us, Lewis observes, a deep well of unfulfilled desire, which we experience as a longing for love, a sense of transcendence, a passion for justice, the exquisite beauty of food or music or wine or sex. But Lewis goes on to notice something else as well: Our deep longings are a well with no bottom, a thirst that's never really quenched.

The books or the music in which we thought the
beauty was located will betray us if we trust to them; it
was not *in* them, it only came *through* them, and what
came through them was longing. . . . For they are not
the thing itself; they are only the scent of a flower we
have not found, the echo of a tune we have not heard,
news from a country we have never yet visited.[13]

In other words, our restlessness, our occasional brushes with transcendence, our vague awareness of spiritual reality, the lostness that we all sooner or later know—all these are signs pointing toward the Home from which we find ourselves displaced. In the words of Lewis's friend and contemporary J. R. R. Tolkien, what we yearn for is "a fleeting glimpse of Joy, Joy beyond the walls of the world, poignant as grief."[14]

EXILE

The Scriptures have a name for this state of affairs: exile.

Six or so centuries before the birth of Jesus of Nazareth, the Jewish people experienced a devastation that forever defined their story. The Babylonian army, in 587 BC or so, besieged and destroyed the city of Jerusalem, then carted off thousands of the surviving Jewish people across hundreds of miles of Middle Eastern desert to a subservient existence in the city of Babylon. The Jewish people in Babylon were far from home, disconnected from everything familiar about their lives. Their city and Temple had been burned, their communities decimated. No home, no future, no hope: They were in exile.

It was, however, in this experience of exile that they edited and gathered into final form the Hebrew Scriptures as we now know them. They told their own story to answer the fundamental human questions we all share: *Who are we?*, *Where are we from?*, and *How did we get here?* And, as they did, they didn't just tell their own story—they told all our stories. They narrated the reality that exile isn't simply the Jewish predicament—it's the human predicament.

In the chapters that begin the Scriptures, humans are created in the image of the living God. They're at home in a creation teeming with goodness, beauty, and harmony (the word *Eden*, the name for the garden home of the first humans, literally means "delight"). The human community is connected to their Creator. They are in harmony with themselves and with one another. The biblical narrator tells us that the primal man and woman "were both naked, and were not ashamed"[15]—in other words, they were both fully vulnerable, fully themselves, and also comprehensively embraced by the other. And the humans were placed in a creation brimming with possibility, called by their Creator to work, create, and develop this good world in which they found themselves.

The far-off country we're made for, our Edenic home, is characterized by what later Hebrew prophets would call shalom. We translate that word into English as "peace," but this is a rather thin and flimsy representation of the fullness the biblical writers depicted. In the words of theologian Cornelius Plantinga Jr., *shalom*, in Scripture, connotes the

> webbing together of God, humans, and all creation in justice, fulfillment, and delight.... Shalom means universal flourishing, wholeness, and delight—a rich state of affairs in which natural needs are satisfied and natural gifts fruitfully employed, all under the arch of God's love. Shalom, in other words, is the way things are supposed to be.[16]

This is, of course, not the world we know. The primeval drama of Genesis 3 depicts humanity turning our backs on our Creator, and in so doing, shalom is violated. Our arrogance ruptures our bonds with God, alienates us from each other, pollutes our relationship to ourselves and to the material world around us. This picture of the wreckage of a world gone wrong is both puzzling and profound.

Look a little closer, for example, at the picture of the human predicament. As God warns the primal people of the effects of taking from the tree of the knowledge of good and evil, he says soberly, "In the day that you eat of it you shall die."[17] But as the narrative unfolds, the humans' rebellion isn't met with death (at least in the way we'd at first assume). Our insurgence issues in banishment. The biblical narrator tells us that "the LORD God sent [the humans] forth from the garden of Eden, to till the ground from which [they were] taken. He drove out the [humans]."[18] Tellingly, across the tapestry of the Hebrew Scriptures, the words used here for God "sending forth" and "driving out" (*shalach* and *garash*, respectively) the man and woman from their Edenic home are used elsewhere to describe the experience of exile.[19] In other words, our banishment from our true Home, our exile from the One we're made for, is the death we all die, every day of our lives, in a world east of Eden.

Then there's the response of the Creator. After they've tasted the forbidden fruit, the man and woman realize they're naked and seek to cover their shame and evade their Maker among the trees of the Garden. This is, obviously, an absurd picture: Shrubbery can't hide humanity from deity. But the biblical narrator tells us that "the LORD God called to the man, and said to him, 'Where are you?'"[20] The first word of God to a vandalized world, and to God's own rebellious children, is not some enraged outburst. God calls into the evening dark like a parent tenderly coaxing a shame-ridden toddler out from hiding under her bed: "Where are you?"

This is God's principal pronouncement to a cosmos gone wrong.

Where are you?

This is the question that echoes around the cosmos.

Where are you?

This is what God keeps asking, as God, in stubborn love, pursues the fickle family of humanity throughout the sprawling drama of the Scriptures.

Where are you?

If you listen hard enough, it's there beneath your longings and your losses, below your brushes with transcendence and glory, between the ordinariness of your everyday and the occasional catastrophes in your story. It resides behind your frantic search for love and acceptance. After it all:

Where are you?

In the exiles of each of our lives, this is the question God is still whispering:

Where are you?

REFLECTION QUESTIONS

1. What are some of the main questions or struggles you've had with believing in God, Christianity, or the church?

2. How have you experienced the longing for Home in your own life?

3. Have you ever sensed God asking *Where are you?* in your life? How do you respond to his voice?

CHAPTER TWO

CURRENTS

The Conditions We're Swimming In

Open your eyes and there it is! By taking a long and thoughtful look at what God has created, people have always been able to see what their eyes as such can't see: eternal power, for instance, and the mystery of his divine being.
ROMANS 1:19-20, MSG

What can be seen on earth points to neither the total absence nor the obvious presence of divinity, but to the presence of a hidden God. Everything bears this mark.
BLAISE PASCAL, *Pensées*

One of our family's favorite haunts in Palm Beach, Florida, is the Jupiter Inlet. A few miles north of our home, the Jupiter Inlet connects the Intracoastal Waterway with an adjacent island of the same name and empties out into the expanse of the Atlantic Ocean. Marinas and waterfront restaurants cluster around its inland side. Families and groups of friends share picnics, swim, barbecue, and play volleyball at the state park along the Intracoastal, and white-sand beachfront stretches toward the horizon north and south from its jetties. On a sunny day, a steady stream of fishing boats, superyachts, and sailboats traffic in and out. The Jupiter Inlet is charming, picturesque, and dangerous.

One morning, as my sons and I cut through the choppy waters of the inlet on a friend's boat en route to fish for red snapper and mackerel off the coast, my friend (whom I'll call Rich), a weathered fishing guide and charter boat captain, told me of the Jupiter Inlet's reputation as one of the most dangerous on the East Coast.

"Why?" I asked. "It doesn't look that dangerous."

"Well," he answered, "you've got to know what's happening under the waterline."

As he angled his flat-bottomed boat out toward the ocean, he nodded toward the north side of the jetty: "This jetty is lined with rocks on both sides, and it's both short and narrow, so there's not a lot of room for error. Big surf breaks at the mouth. And there's a riptide, so there are parts of the day when the tide will be ripping out while big swells are rolling in. On top of that, there's a shoaling sandbar just past the mouth of the inlet a ways. You've always got to pay attention to the conditions. Let's just say that things get treacherous here easily."

The currents swirling and crashing in and out of the Jupiter Inlet are a picture of the power of *conditions*. What's happening in the wind and atmosphere, and what's going on under the waterline, beneath the level of our direct attention, are often outside our explicit awareness. These factors can wind up affecting and directing us—even shipwrecking us. This is true on the water, and I believe it's true as we navigate life as well.

This book is a meditative conversation on the Christian story—a guided tour of the faith for the skeptical and the curious, the jaded and the disaffected. If you're here looking for a philosophical dissertation or some systematic saber rattling on the existence of God, you will look in vain. However, I do think it's wise to pay attention to the conditions. So before proceeding to discuss the Christian drama directly, I want to pause to attend to the cultural conditions in which those of us who inhabit the global West in the twenty-first century are immersed. It's often the under-the-waterline dynamics, behind and beneath our explicit beliefs or conscious awareness, that make it difficult to hear the Voice calling us Home.

RISE OF THE "NONES"

To begin with, we all live in the stream of a steady, barely noticeable undercurrent: the general loss of widespread religious faith in the global West. This gradual but continual reality has exerted its pull on Western societies for the last several centuries. In 2015, the Pew Research Center released the results of a large-scale study charting the continual decline of religious observance in America. The headline-making findings of the study charted the "rise of the 'nones'"—those adults who claim no religious affiliation[1]. Just a few years later, Pew noted that, for the first time, three in ten adults in the US are now religiously unaffiliated. This percentage of the public "is 6 percentage points higher than it was five years ago and 10 points higher than a decade ago."[2] What's more, "nones" have become the largest single affiliation in Pew's religious studies in the US today.[3]

The philosopher Charles Taylor, in his book *A Secular Age*, maps the terrain of the modern West and charts several centuries of intellectual and social history by which we have arrived at the trends we currently experience. Oftentimes, he notes, we assume an implicit "subtraction story" when it comes to modern skepticism. In other words, we presume that "human beings [have] lost, or sloughed off, or liberated themselves from certain earlier, confining horizons, or illusions, or limitations of knowledge."[4] The inference is that several centuries of scientific and technological development have "subtracted" the need for God from the concerns of life. We can subtract the need for God to explain the existence of the universe, for example. We have the sciences for that. We can subtract dependence on the supernatural for life's crises. We have modern medicine to cure our ills and modern technology to solve our problems.

Taylor demonstrates that this "subtraction story" is illusory; modern secularism is a complex nexus of beliefs no more empirically provable on its own than any other view of the world. And yet for many this creates a powerful (and often unseen) pull. As a result, modern Western people tend to assume that secular people live according to purely scientific, rational beliefs while those who are religious live by faith—and by "faith" we mean religious or optimistic feelings unconnected to reason or facts.

Lesslie Newbigin, a Christian theologian and church leader who spent his life working in both India and his native England, draws on the work of several sociologists in observing that no person or human community arrives at their ultimate beliefs by "pure" reason or rationality. Rather, Newbigin observes, all human communities live within socially constructed "plausibility structures." A plausibility structure is

> a social structure of ideas and practices which creates the conditions which determine whether or not a belief

> is plausible. To hold beliefs which fall outside this plausibility structure is to be a heretic in the original sense of the word *haeresis*, that is to say, one who makes his own decisions.[5]

In other words, it isn't just those of us who turn up to houses of worship or espouse belief in the divine who live by faith. All human communities live together according to some web of unprovable tenets. We're all creatures of faith, like it or not.

In the context of Western culture over the last several centuries, this means that, for more and more people, the Christian faith is outside their plausibility structure—the socially accepted and implicitly assumed network of beliefs, cultural formation, and social connections in which they live their lives. And so the person who undertakes a substantive exploration of the Christian story must be willing to become a *heretic*—a blasphemer of the dull orthodoxies of modern skepticism.

PROJECTION

In the climate conditions of contemporary life, it is commonplace to assume that belief in God is nothing more than an exercise in wish fulfillment. To depict this, philosophers sometimes employ the analogy of someone wandering in a desert, racked with thirst.[6] A solitary wanderer crosses yet another mound of sand. She's blasted by a merciless wind and withering under the sun. Swallowing her saliva isn't doing anything to assuage her cotton mouth. But then, in the distance, along a hazy horizon, she sees it: an oasis. Water. Life. But, as she stumbles forward and summons her ebbing strength to push on, she slowly realizes that what she thinks she's seen is a hallucination: Her thirst for water has played a cruel trick on her eyes. Her dehydration does not a fresh spring in the desert make.

Often we assume that this dynamic is what's at work in people of faith. We long for transcendence and meaning and so conjure up God or gods of one sort or another. We wish for immortality, so we invent eternal life. We crave coherence and purpose and so dutifully adhere to our religious systems. But really, this is all just a projection, writ large, of our own wishing. Sigmund Freud, the father of contemporary psychoanalysis, puts it this way: For him, religious beliefs were "illusions, fulfilments of the oldest, strongest and most urgent wishes of mankind. The secret of their strength lies in the strength of those wishes."[7]

As our desert wanderer painfully discovers, desiring something doesn't mean it's there. She may thirst for water, but that thirst doesn't mean there's a spring to be found. Or to mix metaphors: I show up at my city's beach on a Saturday morning, watch the figures bobbing on boards out beyond the breaking waves, and want to do what they're doing. I may dream of being able to surf—of knowing the thrill of dropping into a wave at just the right moment, of carving my way up and down the ocean's curl—but my pining to become a surfer doesn't somehow transform me into Kelly Slater or Kai Lenny.

Oxford scientist and theologian Alister McGrath discusses this theory of religious phenomena, stating that "the Great Projection Theory . . . declares that we have fallen into the habit of projecting our hopes and longings onto some imaginary supernatural screen, and believing that the result is as real as the world of sense and experience."[8]

But here's the catch: The Great Projection Theory assumes that the having of desires makes them untrue or unreliable. All longings, this theory suggests, are by nature mirages. All it takes is turning this assertion around and looking at it carefully from the other end for us to realize its shortcoming.

On the one hand, our desert wanderer's thirst doesn't in and of itself mean that there's an oasis in the distance. And yet her thirst does not, on the other hand, mean that there is no such thing as H_2O. On the contrary: She feels the dryness of her thirst because she needs water to live. The having of our deep desires doesn't, on its own, mean they're real, but it also doesn't signify that they're not. In fact, we experience the desires that drive us because they drive us to our truest and deepest needs—food, water, oxygen, hope, love. As we learn to trust the testimony of our core longings, we discover that they invite us to the Voice that quietly, persistently beckons.

HIDDEN PRESENCE

So does God exist simply because we want God to exist? Is there any way to *know* that God exists? To prove it, in other words? The effort to "prove" the existence or character of God has a long, and mixed, history in Christian thought.[9] To my mind, efforts to construct an airtight rational argument for the existence of God inevitably come off as convincing to some (notably, those ready to be convinced) and less so to the rest of us. Blaise Pascal was a brilliant seventeenth-century French mathematician, physicist, philosopher, and writer. In 1654, after his father fell gravely ill, he experienced the beginnings of what became a dramatic, and intense, conversion to the Christian faith. Several years later, he penned his *Pensées*, or "*Thoughts*," on Christianity, in which he observes that

> what can be seen on earth points to neither the total absence nor the obvious presence of divinity, but to the presence of a hidden God. Everything bears this mark.[10]

I think Pascal's pronouncement strikes the right note. On the one hand, there's no airtight argument by which someone might be intellectually strong-armed into believing the Christian claims about God. On the other hand, in my experience, the thoughtful, skeptical people I've interacted with through the years also want to know that it's not *irrational* to trust themselves to the Christian faith either. They want to know that there are good reasons to believe the Good News they're drawn to—to know that their faith is *warranted*:[11] intellectually and existentially honest and justified. As Pascal notes in *Pensées*, it is ultimately often the experiential coherence and beauty of the Christian faith that ultimately draw people to embrace the gospel. Many of us, however, do want to see that Christianity is *reasonable* before we can experience it as *beautiful*.

So I happily concede that there's no unassailable argument capable of intellectually wrestling someone into belief. And I remind you that the book you hold in your hands doesn't pretend to offer any ivory-tower philosophizing. That said, there are many mysteries to the state of affairs we call life in this cosmos for which intelligent people have concluded the best explanation is that there is indeed a living God—that we're not alone in this vast existence.

For starters, there is the mystery that there is something

rather than nothing. Most scientists agree that our physical universe began with a surge of energy often nicknamed the "big bang" some billions of years ago and that all life as we know it has developed from that initial beginning. But this begs a couple of questions: Where did that initial energy come from? How could nothing have created something? Francis Collins, a geneticist who for years led the Human Genome Project, put it this way on one occasion when he was interviewed about his faith:

> I can't imagine how nature, in this case the universe, could have created itself. And the very fact that the universe had a beginning implies that someone was able to begin it. And it seems to me that had to be outside of nature. And that sounds like God.[12]

In addition to the mystery of our beginnings, there's the puzzle of our mutual ethical obligations. Even the most skeptical of my friends often feel an acute sense of justice: that all people ought to be treated with fairness, regardless of their tax bracket or gender or skin color. That the strong ought to help the weak instead of crushing them. That using one's power to abuse another is wicked. And yet these same friends live with a view of the world that says that there is no ultimate, objective standard of justice or injustice, right or wrong, and that all our actions are finally meaningless and random.

C. S. Lewis, in his *Mere Christianity*, discusses his own puzzlings over the same problem. He writes that, for many years, the immense and seemingly senseless wickedness in the world led him to think that a good God simply couldn't exist. "But then," Lewis writes, "that threw me back into another difficulty." He continues,

> My argument against God was that the universe seemed so cruel and unjust. But how had I got this idea of *just* and *unjust*? A man does not call a line crooked unless he has some idea of a straight line. What was I comparing this universe with when I called it unjust? . . . Of course I could have given up my idea of justice by saying it was nothing but a private idea of my own. But if I did that, then my argument against God collapsed too—for the argument depended on saying that the world was really unjust, not simply that it did not happen to please my fancies. Thus in the very act of trying to prove that God did not exist—in other words, that the whole of reality was senseless—I found I was forced to assume that one part of reality—namely my idea of justice—was full of sense. Consequently atheism turns out to be too simple.[13]

We're outraged at the injustice and rottenness of the world. We shake our fists at the heavens. But, as Lewis perceives, our very notions of good and evil are themselves a window through which we glimpse the Goodness we're made for.

Then there's the mystery of beauty. Imagine that it's December, so you attend a performance of Handel's *Messiah*. And though you don't believe a lick of any of the Scripture passages that constitute its text, to your surprise, the oratorio stirs you in a deep way. Or you spend an afternoon wandering the Musée National Marc Chagall in Nice, France. As you meander through the collection of canvas paintings, stained-glass creations, and sculptures, you're transfixed by the modernist master's energetic, almost frantic lines and vivid use of color. What to make of this? Someone who is committed to thoroughgoing secularism will insist that phenomena like beauty are nothing more than the products of neurons firing in the brain, biochemical reactions. And yet I don't know anyone, believer or no, who lives their life this way.

We confront the same conundrum as we try to make sense of love. My wife appreciates it when I tell her that I love her and think her a beautiful woman. She'd be considerably uninspired, I suspect, if on our wedding anniversary I handed her a card that read, "Honey, my nervous system is reacting to the data my senses have collected about your bodily appearance and your particular odor in a way that produces the chemical reactions in the cortex of my brain that we commonly associate with love." Regardless of our ultimate beliefs, we all live as if beauty, meaning, and love actually exist. *So: Where did they come from?*

And with those mysteries in mind, we'll leave the philosophers behind. After all, being a Christian, at bottom, isn't mainly a matter of giving your intellectual assent to a set of propositions. God isn't a hypothetical idea to be agreed to but Someone to be known, a Glory to be experienced, a Love with whom to commune.

HEARING THE VOICE

One of my favorite indie rock songwriters is the musician David Bazan. His catalog across the years, both as front man of the band Pedro the Lion and in his solo work, charts his journey from his struggles with the fundamentalist faith he inherited from his family to his eventual loss of belief. His 2009 album *Curse Your Branches* constitutes his formal breakup with institutional Christianity. It explores, with unrelenting honesty, Bazan's struggles with Christian teaching regarding the origins of sin, his revulsion at the church's sundry sex scandals, his skepticism about supposed proofs for the Christian faith, and more.

On one sticky August evening, I made my way to Philadelphia's First Unitarian Church to see him in concert. David Bazan performed in the basement of "The Church," as concertgoers have nicknamed it, that night for several hours. He played his way around his early Pedro the Lion catalog and straight through to the searing songs comprising *Curse Your Branches*. Between songs, he'd often take questions from audience members and hold forth on his own disillusionment. Finally, at the end of the evening, he closed his set with a heartbreakingly honest number titled "In Stitches." As he sang about wrestling with drinking to numb his spiritual struggles and fielding his daughter's searching questions about God, he compared himself to a crew who has killed their captain but can still hear his voice.[14]

The wrenching honesty I heard in Bazan's voice that night is a picture of the conditions in which we find ourselves. The currents of the twenty-first-century West in which we're immersed would claim there's no Captain after all. Or that our technological advances, our sophistication, and our supposed enlightenment have killed off any primitive need we once had for one.

But: Listen more deeply to the mysteries of life. Savor more deeply the beauty and meaning and love you've tasted. Look a bit longer at the sorrow and outrage, at the injustice and villainy, that greet us daily on the news, in our neighborhoods, and around the globe. Look. Taste. Listen. You may just hear an echo of the Voice we assumed was gone all along.

REFLECTION QUESTIONS

1. How do you think your relationships, cultural surroundings, and experiences have shaped how you approach spirituality or God?

2. This chapter discusses how all of us are "creatures of faith," whether we believe in God or not. Do you think this is true? If so, how do you notice this in your own life?

3. What are some ways you sense a hidden "echo of [a] Voice" in your life?

CHAPTER THREE

YHWH

Discovering God

> *Through the fire and through the flames*
> *You won't even say your name*
> *Only "I Am That I Am"*
> *But who could ever live that way?*
> *Ut Deo, Ya Hey*
> *Ut Deo, Deo*
>
> **VAMPIRE WEEKEND,** "Ya Hey"

Some time ago, I read a story about a six-year-old Scottish girl named Lulu.[1] She arrived home from school one day and decided to write a letter to God:

To God
how did you get invented?

From Lulu xo

Lulu's father, British journalist Alex Renton, is an atheist, but he wanted to honor little Lulu's curiosity, so he emailed the letter to several Christian friends and family members—and, for good measure, sent it to the heads of several UK church bodies. The Scottish Episcopal Church didn't reply, and neither did the Presbyterian Church. The office of the Scottish Catholic Church sent back some dense theological abstractions. But a couple of weeks later, Renton received an email from "Archbishop Rowan" (Rowan Williams, then archbishop of Canterbury and head of the Anglican Communion) addressed to Lulu:

> *Dear Lulu,*
> *Your dad has sent on your letter and asked if I have any answers. It's a difficult one! But I think God might reply a bit like this—*
>
>> "Dear Lulu—Nobody invented me—but lots of people discovered me and were quite surprised. They discovered me when they looked round at the world and thought it was really beautiful or really mysterious and wondered where it came from. They discovered me when they were very very quiet on their own and felt a sort of peace and love they hadn't expected.
>> Then they invented ideas about me—some of them sensible and some of them not very sensible. From time to time I sent them some hints—specially in the life of Jesus—to help them get closer to what I'm really like.
>> But there was nothing and nobody around before me to invent me. Rather like somebody who writes a story in a book, I started making

up the story of the world and eventually
invented human beings like you who could ask
me awkward questions!"

And then he'd send you lots of love and sign off.
I know he doesn't usually write letters, so I have to do
the best I can on his behalf. Lots of love from me too.

+Archbishop Rowan

Archbishop Rowan's wise, kind words to Lulu get at the heart of what Christians believe: that Christ shows us what the invisible God is really like. Jesus of Nazareth is our decisive picture of the almighty One. In poetry and prose, songs and letters, the earliest Christians say this with one voice.

The Gospel of John begins with an exalted prologue whose rhythmic poetry was likely an early Christian hymn. John draws together the Creation and Exodus stories from the Hebrew Scriptures and brings the Hebrew wisdom tradition and Greek philosophy into a unified symphonic poetry.[2] At its crescendo, John trumpets:

No one has ever seen God; it is God the only Son, ever
at the Father's side, who has revealed Him.[3]

Christ, the Word of God, as John describes him, is God's full self-expression; Christ is how God has spoken to the world once and for all. And Christ "reveal[s]" God; he "ma[kes] him known," as some English translations put it.[4]

Christians have been singing this from our earliest days. The book of Colossians, for example, quotes what most scholars think is likely a very early hymn. It would have been sung at some of the budding gatherings of believers. It portrays Christ as

> the [visible] image of the invisible God, the firstborn of all creation. . . . For in him all the fullness of God was pleased to dwell, and through him God was pleased to reconcile to himself all things.[5]

It is in the narrative of Jesus of Nazareth that we come to get a fuller glimpse of the unseen Creator. And we might add, too, that coming to comprehend Christ Jesus also involves entering the larger narrative of the Hebrew people within which Jesus lived. It's in this sprawling Story, old as the world and expansive as the universe, that Christians are audacious enough to say we can know our unknowable Creator.

MAKER OF HEAVEN AND EARTH

To begin at the beginning:

> In the beginning . . . God created the heavens and the earth.[6]

Christians believe that God, who was unveiled to the world through Christ, is the Maker of all things. The beginning chapters of the book of Genesis feature soaring, rhythmic verse depicting God shaping an ordered cosmos brimming with beauty, harmony, and possibility out of vacant nothingness. Many contemporary people reading the opening chapters of the book that begins the Bible get mired in arguments about our ancient origins or the age of our planet, about fossil records and carbon dating. These squabbles miss the point entirely.

The primeval poetry that begins the Bible intends to introduce us to the character of our Maker. As one statement of faith from my own tradition puts it, "the universe [including the Genesis depiction of its creation] . . . is before our eyes like a beautiful book in which all creatures, great and small, are as letters to make us ponder the invisible things of God."[7] The "book of creation" draws us to contemplate the Creator.

The picture of the Almighty that comes into view in the rhythms of the biblical Creation narrative is of a God who is powerful, artful, and *good*. This comes into especially sharp relief when you read the Genesis account of Creation against the backdrop of the other ancient Near Eastern origin stories with which the Israelites would have been conversant. Historians and archaeologists have recovered several creation myths that the Jewish people in their exilic conditions would have known. Many biblical scholars have concluded that the biblical account of Creation in Genesis 1 and 2 is written as a counternarrative to the creation myths of the Jews' pagan neighbors. When reading them alongside one another, one certainly notices parallels of form and genre. But there are dramatic differences in how Genesis depicts God and his creation and how the other stories portray their deities.[8]

The Enuma Elish, for example, was the creation myth in circulation among the Babylonian Empire, in which the Israelites lived. In it, the creation of the world proceeds from the Babylonian god Marduk defeating Tiamat, a primeval sea goddess. Marduk cuts Tiamat in two pieces; the Tigris and

Euphrates Rivers issue from her eyes, the mountains are shaped from her breasts, and the heavens emerge from her nether regions. Marduk creates humanity after killing the god Kingu (Tiamat's lover) and mixing his blood with sand. Humans in the Enuma Elish are formed so that they might do menial labor that allows the gods to rest.

Then there's the Akkadian Atrahasis epic, which narrates the story of the Sumerian gods and their creation of the world. Some of the lesser gods (the Igigi) rebel against the seven greater gods (the Anunna) because they are being burdened with labor. Before a battle ensues, they reach a peaceful compromise: They'll create mankind to do work for them. All sides agree, and they slaughter the god Aw-ilu, mingling his flesh and blood with clay to make humanity. In these mythologies and the others on offer in the ancient Near East, the point is clear (and bleak): Violence and domination are at the heart of life. The world is a dark place. Human life is utilitarian—we exist to placate angry kings and gods and to discharge servile duties.

> **In the biblical depiction, reality doesn't issue from power and pettiness and violence. The Maker doesn't birth the world into being out of ego or lack or vengeance. Creation, we might say, was simply the kind of thing the living Creator would do.**

Now Genesis. In the biblical depiction, reality doesn't issue from power and pettiness and violence. The Maker doesn't birth the world into being out of ego or lack or vengeance. Creation, we might say, was simply the kind of thing the living Creator would do. The theologian Cornelius Plantinga Jr. puts it like this:

Creation is neither a necessity nor an accident. Instead, given God's interior life that overflows with regard for others, we might say creation is an act that was *fitting* for God. It was so much *like* God to create, to imagine possible worlds and then to actualize one of them. Creation is an act of imaginative love.[9]

The one God speaks, and at God's word, life springs into being.[10] God's generating word showcases divine imagination, peaceful power, and patient care. Over untold eons, God makes, forms. He contours shape and form where there is void and fills a universe with life where there is only emptiness and nothingness. God's creating is staggering and expansive: heavens and earth, land and sea. And it's meticulously intricate: the roughly 435,000 species of land plants,[11] the over one million species of insects,[12] the between one and two million different species of animals.[13] God's originating work issues from his goodness, and goodness pulses at the very heart of reality. The steady rhythm of *It was good* punctuates the Genesis Creation account, and God concludes his creating work by blessing and pronouncing benediction upon the infant world: "God saw everything that he had made, and indeed, it was very good."[14]

In the Genesis story, human life isn't a product of violence or the lust of the gods for slave labor. Humans are created to bear the image of their Creator. And it isn't, as was the case for Israel's pagan neighbors, only kings, or only male human beings, who bear the divine mark. In the Genesis story, *all* people bear God's image. Humans aren't brought into being as slave labor but to commune with God, know one another, and steward the beauty and possibility of the good creation.

This is the God whom the "book of creation" unveils; this is the invisible One for whom Jesus Christ is the visible image. No wonder, then, that in the Scriptures, the appropriate response to the doctrine of Creation isn't academic wrangling or speculative conjecture but fullhearted worship:

Praise the LORD! . . .

Praise him, sun and moon;
    praise him, all you shining stars!
Praise him, you highest heavens,
    and you waters above the heavens!

Let them praise the name of the LORD,
    for he commanded and they were created.[15]

GOD'S FAMILY STORY

Once when I was being interviewed for a podcast, the host began our conversation with a question borrowed from the poet Thomas Lynch. Lynch's ten-syllable question, asked in iambic pentameter, is this: "How do we come to be the ones we are?"[16] Put less poetically, my interviewer was asking me, "Who are you?"

Interestingly, as I answered, my instinct was to tell the story of my family and the significant relationships that have formed me through my years—my wife, close friends, colleagues, and children. As I thought about this later, it brought home to me just how deeply we are formed by our families and circles of relationships. Non-Western cultures that are less steeped in individualism know this truth deeply. Jared Ayers is unknowable and irrelevant apart from the stories of the Ayers and Zeiset families and the interconnected web of human contact I've shared in across my life.

In the same way, when someone reads the Scriptures to discover more about God, she quickly finds herself reading family stories—in particular, the history of the Jewish people. One of the most frequent handles with which God expresses himself is "the God of Abraham, the God of Isaac, and the God of Jacob."[17] The living God has a story, a family. And knowing the God disclosed in Jesus means entering these ancient family stories.

Following the elegant stories of Creation in Genesis 1 and 2, we encounter the primordial story of paradise lost that begins in Genesis 3. And as one reads the next eight chapters of the Bible, one sees primeval depictions of the way human rottenness spoils God's good creation in ever more ruinous ways. But in Genesis 12 there's a new beginning, and this is where the family stories of Israel get their start: with Abraham.

After a genealogy depicting humanity's spread around Mesopotamia, Genesis 12 begins abruptly:

> Now the LORD said to Abram, "Go from your country and your kindred and your father's house to the land that I will show you. I will make of you a great nation, and I will bless you, and make your name great, so that you will be a blessing. I will bless those who bless you, and the one who curses you I will curse; and in you all the families of the earth shall be blessed."[18]

God speaks to Abram—whose name is later changed to Abraham—residing in Haran (probably modern-day Turkey), and calls him to leave everything he's ever known for an unknown destination and an undisclosed future. God commits himself to this person and his as-yet-nonexistent family and announces that he will work through Abraham and his family to bring flourishing to the whole world: "In you all the families of the earth shall be blessed."

The word *bless* is used five times in these three verses, and in the narrative structure of the book, these are a deliberate counterpoint to the five "cursings" contained in Genesis 3 through 11 (Genesis 3:14, 17; 4:11; 8:21; 9:25). In other words, God intimates here that he's chosen to act through the human family, such as it is, to renew and repair his entire sin-ravaged creation.

We can know the living God, these ancient family stories tell us, not only via the expanse of our universe but also because the Creator has chosen to make binding commitments of relationship to humanity. In the language of faith, we call these promises God's covenant commitments. A covenant was a common sort of relational agreement in the ancient world; it was "a bond in blood sovereignly administered."[19] Covenants bound two parties in a relationship with one another. And they regularly included both promises and demands on the part of each party.

We hear this in God's summons. There are promises—such as "I will make of you a great nation," "I will . . . make your name great," and "You will be a blessing"—and a demand: Abraham is summoned to depart his own environs and to follow the voice addressing him. He's entering a new way of life. As Lesslie Newbigin observes, "Here is the beginning of a new kind of human living, one that does not depend on the securities we have accumulated over the past, but depends wholly on what God has promised for the future. A new kind of life—living by faith."[20] The divine summons that Abraham is given is to now live by faith—to enter a life of active, and often risky, trust in this unseen God.

So what's so special about Abraham? As you follow his and his family's stories, the answer is, on the surface of it, nothing. Abraham's not especially devout or moral, and he often doesn't even seem to trust God all that much. He and his children regularly engage in all sorts of trickery, pettiness, and violence.

One time several years ago, as I was walking off the pitch after playing a rugby match, a teammate named Jeff, who had just discovered that I was a Christian and a pastor, announced to me: "Hey! Jared! You should know that I started reading the Bible for the first time this week." He went on to tell me that the girl he was currently dating, being from a Roman Catholic family, had recently dragged him to a Mass service on Ash Wednesday, and they had decided that the "good deed" they were going to commit to together would be to start reading the Bible. He told me that he had made it through a little more than half the book of Genesis.

"Well, what do you think so far?" I asked.

"I'm gonna be honest," Jeff said, as he wiped the sleeve of his jersey across his forehead to remove a clump of dirt still left from the match. "There's some crazy stuff in the Bible. All those Abraham stories—that guy seems terrible. Pretends his wife is his sister. Gets his servant or slave or whatever pregnant and then sends her away. His kids are a debacle too."

Jeff went on to ask me if Abraham was supposed to be some example of an especially religious or devout person and why his story was in a book that claimed to be in some way from God. And so, over our post-match stretch, I told him that he'd gotten the point, even if he didn't realize it: that these stories show us God doggedly determining to be faithful to fickle, dysfunctional, and blemished people—in other words, people like us.

And it's this paradox that's shot through all the narratives and poetry, prose, and prophecy that constitute the Hebrew Scriptures: The family God has committed himself to rescue the world through are deeply flawed themselves. They're in need of rescue, just like the whole lot of humanity. As Rabbi Lionel Blue once said, "Jews are just like everyone else, only more so."[21]

All of us children of Abraham, it turns out, are pretty much a debacle.

"YA HEY"

The signature moment in the Hebrew Scriptures in which we get a glimpse of God transpires generations after Abraham's time, near the outset of the Exodus story. Abraham's family tree has grown into an honest-to-goodness people group. But the Hebrews are languishing in slavery, under the thumb of the Egyptian Empire. One of their number, Moses, after being rescued from certain death as an infant, is raised in the halls of

Egyptian power as the adopted son of the pharaoh's daughter. But as a young man, Moses watches as one of his own people is brutally beaten by an Egyptian taskmaster. In an outburst of anger, Moses murders the Egyptian, and once word gets out, he becomes a fugitive from the rage of the pharaoh.

Four long decades later, Moses has settled into life as a fugitive, has married, and lives a world away from his people and all that he used to know. Exodus 3 tells us that at the time of Moses' decisive encounter with the Almighty, he is "beyond the wilderness."[22] One day, as Moses accompanies his flock through the wilderness, he sees something strange: a bush blazing with divine brilliance that's somehow not being consumed by its own fire. Moses moves closer, and as he does, God calls: "Moses, Moses!"

God informs Moses that he's on holy ground and goes on to announce that he's heard the desperate cries of the Israelites, that he knows their pain, and that he's going to emancipate them from their cruel slavery. And that Moses will be leading them.

Moses balks. And as he protests, he asks, "If I come to the Israelites and say to them, 'The God of your ancestors has sent me to you,' and they ask me, 'What is his name?' what shall I say to them?" In response, the voice declares:

I Am Who I Am.[23]

The invisible God here declares God's Name. But fascinatingly, this is a name that's also not really a name:

"Who are you?"

"I Am."

Berkeley Hebrew Bible scholar Robert Alter says of this exchange that "God's response perhaps gives Moses more than he bargained for—not just an identifying divine name . . . but an ontological divine mystery of the most daunting character. Rivers of ink have since flowed in theological reflection on and philological analysis of this name."²⁴

He's right. This interchange has been, over millennia, studied, prayed, meditated upon, dissected, analyzed. Here's an approximation of the vast quantity of thinking and praying about what's disclosed here to Moses—and, by extension, to the rest of us.

The divine disclosure in Exodus 3 can be translated as I AM WHO I AM or I WILL BE WHO I WILL BE. The living God is not an object to be studied, a force to be wielded, an idea to be argued. God will not be managed, pinned down, coerced, cornered. God is Life. God is Being. God is Mystery. God is wholly and entirely Other from us.

The Name is formed from the Hebrew verb for "to be," *hayah*, and the characters of that word form the title God goes on to use in the next sentence: "Thus you shall say to the Israelites, 'The LORD [YHWH], the God of your ancestors . . . has sent me to you.'"²⁵

This divine Name, most scholars agree, would have been pronounced "Yahweh"²⁶ and would have formed the personal name for God that came to predominate usage in the Hebrew Scriptures. In older translations of the English Bible, *YHWH* was translated *Jehovah*; in current ones, it's signified wherever English Bibles translate "Lord" (in small caps) for the Name of God. *YHWH* is "used 6,700 times in the Old Testament as compared to the 2,500 occurrences of the generic Semitic term for divinity, *Elohim*."[27] The living God is not far off, aloof, and cranky. God is personal, knowable. We can't use God or control God, but we can address God, know God, be known by God.

There's more. The four Hebrew letters that constitute the Name—*yod, hay, waw, hay*—are also associated with breath. When vocalized, they make the sounds of a person's inhale and exhale. For the Hebrews, breath was the very essence of life. In the Creation story, the Lord of the universe—Life itself—"breathed into [the man's] nostrils the breath of life; and the man became a living being."[28] A Jewish prayer book teaches, "The breathing of all life, praises your Name, YHWH our Elohim."[29] God is beyond us; God is wholly Other. And God is also Near. The staggering claim of Holy Scripture is that the God of the universe is as close to you and me as the breath in our own lungs.

The band Vampire Weekend captured this paradox in their song "Ya Hey"—itself a riff on the revelatory Name:

> *Through the fire and through the flames*
> *You won't even say your name*
> *Only "I Am That I Am"*
> *But who could ever live that way?*[30]

These lines express the paradox perfectly: God is wholly Other than us; God is Mystery; we can never presume to have defined him or pinned him down as we'd define a word in the dictionary or test some foreign material in a laboratory. God is not just some metaphysical object for us to poke, prod, theorize, and argue about.

And on the other hand, the unknowable, invisible One, the God of the cosmos, has chosen to truly disclose his own self to us, Christians believe, in the story of Israel and eventually in the person of Jesus and the pages of Scripture. This is not, as the Swiss theologian Karl Barth is said to have put it, just "man writ large" but disruptive, divine self-disclosure.

And this is just what so many twenty-first-century people have such a hard time with. In a world with dizzying pluralism, in which people have so many conceptions of God, or the gods, or spiritual reality, isn't it impossibly arrogant, and dangerously divisive, to claim that we have the corner on truth when it comes to the divine? Don't we all really believe in the same thing, more or less, no matter how we think about God or what we choose to call God?

I've had this conversation many, many times with friends and neighbors over the years. And I'll be the first to admit that there's no shortage of impossibly arrogant and dangerously divisive Christians walking this planet. I wish that weren't the case, but I can't pretend it's not so. At the same time, I don't know that it's actually helpful, when confronted with the realities of differing religious beliefs, to just shrug one's shoulders and say, "Well, we're all pretty much talking about the same thing, amiright?"

I say that not just as a pastor or a Christian but as someone who has for years had neighbors and good friends who are Muslim, or Hindu, or Buddhist, and more. If you were to approach one of my friends and say, "What you and Jared believe is all really the same, right?" they'd kindly tell you that no, what we believe is not in fact the same. Boston University professor Stephen Prothero makes this point well:

> No one argues that different economic systems or political regimes are one and the same. Capitalism and socialism are so self-evidently at odds that their differences hardly bear mentioning. The same goes for democracy and monarchy. Yet scholars continue to claim that religious rivals such as Hinduism and Islam, Judaism and Christianity are, by some miracle of the imagination, both essentially the same and basically good. . . .
>
> This is a lovely sentiment but it is untrue, disrespectful, and dangerous.
>
> The gods of Hinduism are not the same as the orishas of Yoruba religion or the immortals of Daoism. To pretend that they are is to refuse to take seriously the beliefs and practices of ordinary religious folk who for centuries have had no problem distinguishing the Nicene Creed of Christianity from the Four Noble Truths of Buddhism from the Shahadah of Islam. . . .
>
> But this lumping of the world's religions into one megareligion is not just false and condescending, it is also a threat. How can we make sense of the ongoing conflict in Kashmir if we pretend that Hinduism and Islam are one and the same? Or of the impasse in the Middle East, if we pretend that there are no fundamental disagreements between Judaism, Christianity and Islam?[31]

Prothero goes on to note that what the various religious traditions of the world have in common is a sense that there's something wrong with the world; but where they diverge is their diagnosis of what that is and who (or Who) might address it. As someone who has lived in communities with a dizzying variety of people with their variety of different beliefs, I think the deepest question isn't *Don't we all really believe the same thing?* but rather *How can we pursue our beliefs about God and meaning in a way that cultivates humility in how we see ourselves and hospitality, generosity, and love in how we live with our neighbors?*

The blazing Glory in the bush dares to disclose that people like me and you, even if we've made a wreck of our lives, can know the Unknowable, behold the Invisible, make contact with the One who is wholly Other. And generations later, a controversial first-century rabbi would be shameless enough to draw on this wilderness encounter in his teachings:

I AM . . .

"the bread of life";
"the light of the world";
"the gate";
"the good shepherd";
"the resurrection and the life";
"the way, and the truth, and the life"; and
"the vine."[32]

The daring announcement at the heart of Christian belief is that, in Jesus—a person like us—the Mystery became mortal;

the invisible One assumed a face, a name, a body; the One who is beyond us came among us.

THREE IN ONE

From the beginnings of the Christian movement, the earliest followers of Jesus held a profound paradox in creative tension. On the one hand, the nascent Christian movement, emerging out of Judaism, continued to be ardently monotheistic: "The LORD our God, the LORD is one."[33] On the other hand, these Christians came to recognize, after Jesus' resurrection from the dead, that the one living God had come to dwell among us in this enigmatic Teacher. What's more, Jesus, before his departure, had spoken mysteriously of God giving his own Spirit to his followers and of both God and him, through this Spirit, somehow giving their intimate and personal presence to Jesus' followers.

And so, from their beginnings, Christians expressed, in various ways, that the word *God* must now somehow include the person Jesus. What's more, the teaching of Jesus himself opens to us a window into God's inner life. According to Jesus, God's Spirit glorifies him; he, in turn, glorifies God the Father; and God the Father glorifies Jesus. This mutual dance of glory, love, and esteem, according to Jesus, has been in motion from eternity past and will pulsate into eternity future.[34] Putting these hints together, Christians realized that the three persons of the one living God exist in a dance of self-giving regard, unconditional affection, and intimate communion.[35]

The shorthand way that subsequent generations in the

church developed to refer to this mystery was in recognizing God as Trinity. After extended reflection, prayer, debate, and eventual consensus, the church came to affirm the following:

There is one God.
Jesus is God.
The Spirit of God is God.

In short: There is one God, who is tripersonal—Father, Son, Holy Spirit. Trinity. The church father Gregory of Nazianzus gathers up the wisdom of the church when he instructs, "Worship the Father and the Son and the Holy Ghost, One Godhead; God the Father, God the Son and . . . God the Holy Ghost, One Nature in Three Personalities, intellectual, perfect, Self-existent, numerically separate, but not separate in Godhead."[36]

Got a handle on all that?

Didn't think so.

Me neither.

Nobody ever really *gets* the Trinity. You can almost hear the sigh of bewilderment from fourth-century bishop Hilary of Poitiers, venturing to teach this topic: "I must undertake something that cannot be limited and venture upon something that cannot be comprehended, so that I may speak about God who cannot be accurately defined."[37]

The Christian teaching on the Trinity explodes our mental and spiritual circuits.

I'll be the first to admit that we're swimming in the deep end of the pool here. But, far from being ethereal or esoteric, the doctrine of the Trinity brims with spiritual and practical meaning. British writer G. K. Chesterton, in his reflections on the Christian faith, recognizes this paradox:

> To us Trinitarians (if I may say it with reverence)—to us God Himself is a society. . . . This triple enigma is as comforting as wine and open as an English fireside; that this thing that bewilders the intellect utterly quiets the heart . . . For it is not well for God to be alone.[38]

Think of the choices we have. If you trust yourself to the secular Western view of life, you consider our existence meaningless—one vast, immense accident ending only in death. So what is at the center of life? Meaninglessness. An absurd few minutes with which you should do whatever you want.

If you're a Christian, you don't have to live within a story of life that says that your life is an incoherent blip in a cosmic void. And you also don't simply believe that there's one God out there somewhere who's powerful or all-knowing. Christians, uniquely, believe that *love* is at the heart of the universe. Why? Because love requires interpersonal relationship. And followers of Jesus are bold enough to say that relationships of love are the very heart of God's interior life. We risk everything on the assertion that the beating heart of all reality, the animating center of all existence, is this: *love*.

THE MEANING IS LOVE

Julian of Norwich was a fourteenth-century medieval anchoress: a woman who spent her life in secluded prayer in a tiny cell of a room. She lived out her days in the English city of

Norwich, enduring devastating sickness for much of her life. At one point, she became so ill that she thought she was on her deathbed, and it was during this time that she experienced several mystical visions of God, which she later recorded in writings gathered and entitled *Revelations of Divine Love*. Her writings are the first published work in the English language by a woman.

Near the end of *Revelations of Divine Love*, Julian describes asking God why she experienced these visions of God's presence and Jesus' suffering. This is the response she records:

> Do you want to know your Lord's meaning in this?
> Be well aware: love was his meaning. Who showed you this? Love. What did he show you? Love. Why did he show it? For love. Hold fast to this, and you will know and understand more of the same; but you will never understand nor know anything else from this for all eternity.[39]

This is the meaning of all God's self-disclosure. This is what's behind our immense, intricate universe, the sprawling narrative of Holy Scripture, and the living, dying, and rising of Jesus, our signature picture of the unseen One.

The meaning is Love.

REFLECTION QUESTIONS

1. Is this discussion of what God is like similar to or different from how you've thought about God before?

2. What are some of the things that Jesus shows us about who God is?

3. Why do Christians believe that love is at the heart of God?

CHAPTER FOUR
MISERABLE OFFENDERS
Our Mutual Predicament

> *I am really just like him*
> *Look beneath the floorboards*
> *For the secrets I have hid*
>
> **SUFJAN STEVENS**, "John Wayne Gacy, Jr."

> *The miserable have no other medicine*
> *But only hope.*
>
> Claudio in **WILLIAM SHAKESPEARE**, *Measure for Measure*

> *Almighty and most merciful Father;*
> *We have erred, and strayed from thy ways like lost sheep.*
> *We have followed too much*
> *the devices and desires of our own hearts. . . .*
> *and there is no health in us.*
> *But thou, O Lord,*
> *Have mercy upon us,*
> *miserable offenders.*
>
> **THE BOOK OF COMMON PRAYER**

When I lived in Philadelphia, my daily commute from my row house to our church's offices included a walk north on the shady, tree-lined sidewalk along Thirteenth Street in the heart of the city's downtown. During those years, a real estate developer who'd become an acquaintance of mine redeveloped a crumbling century-old building along this storied stretch of city street. This building had housed, for the better part of the prior century, a brothel with a notoriously unsavory reputation. After he'd acquired the rights to the building and repurposed it, this developer opened a sleek cocktail lounge on the ground floor. And in a knowing nod to the property's original purpose, he named the new watering hole Charlie Was a Sinner.

It made me chuckle, walking by the entrance to that speakeasy day after day. I smiled at the irony: Here was this name emblazoned seductively across the awning, displaying for the masses some singularly unfashionable vernacular—*sin, sinner.*

The mere mention of the "*s* word"—*sin*—feels, of course, deeply outdated. The cluster of terms that classical Christianity employs to name the wrong of the world—words like *transgression, wickedness, trespass, misdeed,* and the like—conjure caricatures of red-faced, sweating, finger-wagging preachers. Or Dana Carvey's *Saturday Night Live* "Church Lady" character sketches. We assume sin language to be antiquated at best, downright oppressive at worst. And so we've largely shelved sin speak, save for when we employ the idiom with a wink and a knowing nod. You're more likely today to encounter Christianity's language for human transgression on the dessert section of the menu from that just-opened Sicilian restaurant in your neighborhood than you are to experience it in a meaningful conversation or a probing op-ed.

But here's the thing.

Scrubbing our discourse of sin language doesn't make the ugly realities we know all too well go away. It just cripples our capacity to deal with them. They're still there, lurking under the waterline of our lives. They're still infesting families. They're still polluting relationships. They're still despoiling neighborhoods, organizations, and whole cultures. British writer and philosopher G. K. Chesterton thought that humanity's sinful predicament was so blatantly obvious that he pronounced it "the only part of Christian theology which can really be proved."[1] We all long for a way to recognize and meaningfully address the rot that resides in the world and in our own depths. But we've by and large forgotten any kind of coherent moral vocabulary by which to name and address the foul realities we all see in the news, in our neighborhoods, and, when we're honest, in the mirror.

I'm campaigning for us to relearn this portion of the Christian language that we've mostly mothballed. And I consider this an urgent, vital task. Not because I enjoy scowling and browbeating. But because doing so gives us a language adequate to understand and address the darkness in which we all spend our lives lurching and stumbling.

Actress Phoebe Waller-Bridge created and starred in an award-winning comedy-drama series entitled *Fleabag*, in which she plays the main character, a woman referred to only by the series' title. Fleabag is quick-witted and cynical, and the show follows her as she meanders through an aimless life, attempting to navigate friendship and love. Her life is utterly devoid of any romantic or sexual restraint. She seems free, but Fleabag also bears a crushing burden of grief and shame. In the finale of the show's first season, Fleabag has a flashback revealing that she slept with the boyfriend of Boo, her best friend, and in so doing, contributed to her friend's accidental death. The final scene finds Fleabag sitting in the café she and Boo used to run together, now dark and empty except for her and a bank manager. He stopped by to meet with Fleabag about the small-business loan for which she'd applied. But as they sit across from one another in her now-vacant, dark shop, Fleabag loses it. Her deep well of shame erupts as she confesses to this stranger: "Everyone feels like this just a little bit and they're not talking about it!"[2]

The Christian story enables us to come to terms with the mutual misery we all feel. To actually be able to coherently talk about it. And, ultimately, it trumpets to us how the God we're made for has done something about it.

OLD GODS, NEW NAMES

What many people envision when they hear the word *sin* is roughly any enjoyable action that religions arbitrarily declare out-of-bounds. I saw a picture of this watching *The Simpsons* one night with my sons. In one episode, Lisa Simpson goes looking for Maggie, her little sister, who's gone missing. She winds up infiltrating a convent of nuns who have unwittingly taken in little Maggie. As Lisa wanders the convent, she passes by a window as a nun teaches a room full of toddlers a nursery rhyme: "If you're happy and you know it—that's a sin! If you're happy and you know it—that's a sin!"[3]

Our assumptions miss the subtlety and sophistication in the way the Christian faith diagnoses the human ailment if we're willing to hear it. Take a minute and read, for example, the Ten Commandments[4]—the text that lies at the center of both Jewish and Christian ethical teaching, and probably the most universally recognizable list of "Thou shalt nots" in the world. What do you notice?

Well, for starters, they're not long. The Ten Commandments are blunt injunctions. In fact, in the Hebrew language in which they were originally written down, several of them contain only two words and comprise just three syllables: "no kill"; "no steal"; "no covet."[5] They'd be easily "memorizable by even the simplest nomad, his ten fingers a constant reminder of [the Ten's] centrality in his life."[6]

Where do the "Ten Words"[7] start? Not where we think. They don't begin by forbidding adultery or outlawing murder. The Ten Words take aim, first and foremost, at our *worship*:

> I am the LORD your God, who brought you out of the land of Egypt, out of the house of slavery; you shall have no other gods before me.
>
> You shall not make for yourself an idol, whether in the form of anything that is in heaven above, or that is on the earth beneath, or that is in the water under the earth. . . .
>
> You shall not make wrongful use of the name of the LORD your God, for the LORD will not acquit anyone who misuses his name.[8]

These commands strike us as strange when we read them in the twenty-first century. But this is what's fascinating: The Ten don't command us to worship or to believe—they assume we already do. They command us to reverence only the living God, rather than false gods. Here's what those primordial tablets of teaching know: It's not only those of us who come to religious sanctuaries, sing songs, and pray prayers who are worshipers. All of us, inescapably, are worshipers.

And it's not just backward, obscure tribal peoples from long ago, whittling shapes out of stone and wood, who worship idols. The word *worship* means, literally,

> *worth* (as in, "value") + *-ship* ("quality") = to value the quality of something or someone.⁹

In other words, to worship is to give your ultimate allegiance, your deepest awed reverence, to something or someone. In that sense, all of us are worshipers.

The question isn't *whether* you'll be a worshiper; it's *whom* or *what* you will worship.

And the root of the human predicament, according to the wisdom of Christian teaching, isn't that we break some archaic, random laws handed down from on high by a disgruntled deity. Our fundamental dilemma is that we all, in our own ways, look for love and security and acceptance elsewhere from the God who is our Home. We center our deepest selves elsewhere from the One we're made for.

Our fundamental dilemma is that we all, in our own ways, look for love and security and acceptance elsewhere from the God who is our Home.

We're idolators.

Theologian Martin Luther, in his writings, notices that when we break one of the seven other commandments of the Big Ten, it's because, at bottom, we're already breaking the first few.[10] Let's say, for example, that I covet my neighbor's wife. Or his Rolex. Or his membership at the club that turned me down last year. Or his stock portfolio. When I do, I'm breaking the tenth commandment. And let's say that I covet his watch or portfolio or club membership or wife enough to try and take those things from him—now I'm also breaking the eighth commandment. What's transpiring on my interior as I do this? Am I just transgressing some artificial, socially conditioned regulation?

All of us with firsthand experience of coveting know that's not it.

My heart lusts for what belongs to my neighbor because, in some subterranean way, I'm looking for security and validation in what I wish I had. I have a coveting problem because I have an idolatry problem. I covet because my worship, the way I direct my deepest affections, is disordered, bent out of shape.

In a provocative essay titled "Idolatry 2.0," N. T. Wright, a leading biblical scholar, notices a parallel between the physical atmosphere and the human psyche: namely that, as the saying goes, "nature abhors a vacuum." Wright explains,

> You can create a vacuum, and you can sustain it given the right technology, but atmospheric pressure always threatens to break back in, sometimes causing an explosion. Well, something similar is true in philosophies and worldviews. They abhor a vacuum. You can push God, or the gods, upstairs out of sight, like an elderly embarrassing relative. But history shows again and again that other gods quietly sneak in to take their place.[11]

Wright goes on to describe several of the gods worshiped in the ancient world. There's Mars, for example—the god of war and military power, also considered the guarantor of security for peoples in an agrarian world. Or Mammon, god of money. Or

Aphrodite, the goddess of sex and erotic love. The ancients, in other words, worshiped sex, money, and power.

Wright notes how, in the modern Western Enlightenment, we've sloughed off all these supposedly backward mythical deities. At the same time, however, there's the fascinating work of the three twentieth-century "masters of suspicion": Friedrich Nietzsche, Karl Marx, and Sigmund Freud. For Freud, human beings are driven in a deep and unconscious way by sex. Human society, claims Marx, is driven by the thirst for money. All of life, according to Nietzsche, is about power. We may think we have complete autonomy and agency over our lives, but for the "masters of suspicion," we are driven by these deep impulses: money, sex, and power. Wright concludes that the ancient gods haven't gone anywhere; we just give the old gods new names, and they're more powerful for being mostly invisible to us.

One of the insights of the Scriptures is that we always come to resemble what we worship. Here's how Psalm 115 depicts this dynamic:

> [Idols] have mouths, but do not speak;
>   eyes, but do not see.
> They have ears, but do not hear;
>   noses, but do not smell.
> They have hands, but do not feel;
>   feet, but do not walk;
>   they make no sound in their throats.
> Those who make them are like them;
>   so are all who trust in them.
> O Israel, trust in the Lord![12]

Did you notice what that ancient hymn observes about idols? It pictures the irony of their impotent unreality—they've got eyes but can't see you, ears but they can't hear your pleadings. It declares, in effect, "They're not real—and when you worship them, your life loses reality." In other words, if we worship the living God—if God is where we seek identity and value and love—our character will come to resemble the Creator's goodness and wisdom and truth. And we will refract God's justice and love out into our relationships, work, and life. But when we worship something or someone other than our Creator—like the approval of a lover or the amassing of stock options—it inevitably deforms us. It dehumanizes us and ultimately destroys the life God intends for us.

GUILT AND POWER

To turn again to the Genesis poetry that begins the Bible's story: In the beginning, the Maker shapes a cosmos brimming with goodness, beauty, delight. But after the humans turn their backs on God, the disease of their tragic betrayal metastasizes to infect the whole creation. The many-sided, primal poetry featured in Genesis 3 depicts sin as having dire spiritual consequences (the humans are alienated from God) as well as psychological ones (they're ashamed, alienated from their true and authentic selves). Sin infests the humans' relationships (domination and subjugation corrupt the human bonds) as well as their vocational life (work will now be a frustration, not only a vocation). Even the material world itself, according to the Bible, is polluted by sin—the soil itself, according to Genesis, bears the curse of our transgression.[13] In the New Testament, Paul picks up on the imagery of Genesis 3—the woman's pains in childbirth, to be exact—to describe the plight of the present world as it awaits God's full, final rescue like a mother groans as she awaits the birth of an infant life she bears in her body: "We know that the whole creation has been groaning in labor pains until now; and not only the creation, but we ourselves . . ."[14]

Almost four centuries ago, English poet John Milton depicted this dynamic in his long-form masterpiece *Paradise Lost*. As he relates the tragedy of the Genesis 3 story in lyric rhythm, Milton writes:

> *. . . her rash hand in evil hour*
> *Forth reaching to the fruit, she plucked, she ate:*
> *Earth felt the wound, and nature from her seat,*
> *Sighing through all her works, gave signs of woe*
> *That all was lost.*[15]

The sober, primeval lines of Genesis, and the poetic retelling they're given by Milton, strike new chords of meaning for us as we read them today. For a half century or more, scientists have urged us to hear the groanings of our planet as human greed has slaked oil reserves and razed forests, human ambition has choked the air with greenhouse gases, and human foolishness has ignored any long-term effects of our actions. Soil, seas, and skies still very much groan over the wounds we've inflicted on the world.

Here's the shorthand way Christians refer to this state of affairs: *misery*. As theologian Cornelius Plantinga Jr. observes, "Sin . . . lies at the root of such big miseries as loneliness, restlessness, estrangement, shame, and meaninglessness. This is . . . why sin is the main human trouble. In fact, sin typically both causes and results from misery."[16]

This way of talking about the human plight holds together a profound paradox: Sin is both a state of affairs in which we are caught up and a situation in which we are culpable, active participants. It encompasses both the ugly things we *do* and the predicament we are *in*. This is why followers of Jesus cry out:

> *Rock of Ages, cleft for me*
> *Let me hide myself in Thee . . .*
> *Be of sin the double cure*
> *Save me from its guilt and power*[17]

Sin, in other words, afflicts humanity as both *guilt* and *power*.[18] We are, all of us, on the one hand, victims—people under the thumb of dark powers in a world gone wrong. And we're also, each of us, offenders—people who contribute, in our own ways, to this profound morass. A classic prayer of confession captures this tension by referring to we who pray it as "miserable offenders."[19] We're mired in the miseries of the human experience, and we are offenders—we contribute to that world of woe in which we're all trapped. As the wizened old preacher in Marilynne Robinson's award-winning novel *Gilead* puts it, "There is never just one transgression. There is a wound in the flesh of human life that scars when it heals and often enough seems never to heal at all."[20]

Many one-sided contemporary analyses by our prominent media figures, politicians, and public intellectuals of what, exactly, wounds the world could use the nuance of this diagnosis. Some see individual responsibility as the root of societal evils: The main problem with the world, according to this way of thinking, is that people make wrong choices and don't take responsibility for their own lives. Others point to the realities of unjust institutions and the widespread systemic evil latent in our communities and nations—racism, sexism, and so on—as the root of what ails us. Unfortunately (and ironically), contemporary Christian voices all too often fall on one side or the other of this simplistic view of life. But the Christian story in its fullness offers us the possibility of moving past these binary reductive alternatives. When asked, "What's the problem with the world? Individuals? Families? Societies? Systems?" Christianity answers, "Yes."

Yes, we are, all of us, victims. And offenders. Miserable offenders.

BENEATH THE FLOORBOARDS

This comprehensive account of our predicament pulls at the roots of our instinctive pride in an unparalleled way. Over the last decades, leading social scientists and cultural theorists have come to affirm what the Bible has long said—that there is lurking in all of us, regardless of ideology, cultural background, or creed, a desperate drive to prove that we're right and good—and especially that we're more right and more righteous than others. Jonathan Haidt, a social scientist and professor at NYU, wrote a book—*The Righteous Mind*—in which he analyzes this phenomenon. The central insight of his extensive research is that "an obsession with righteousness (leading inevitably to self-righteousness) is the normal human condition."[21] This inner

Pharisee is hardwired into our neurological functioning and our social conditioning.

This condition creeps into us all, churchgoing and atheistic, conservative and progressive, old and young alike. And in an increasingly globalized, interconnected, and diverse world, it only intensifies. We all have our "others," as the sociologists say—or, as I often describe the situation, our "those people":

"Those narrow-minded religious people."
"Those atheists."
"Those liberals."
"Those conservatives."
"Those young people."
"Those old people."
"Those uneducated rednecks."
"Those overeducated elites."
"Those Black people."
"Those white people."

But the Christian understanding of our sinfulness emphasizes that all people, all communities, all societies share in the universal dilemma, regardless of creed, class, or ideology. This awareness shapes a dignified humility in how I see myself and how I see others, especially those whom I tend to treat as "those people."

My colleagues and family members and the neighbor across the street whom I think is deeply mistaken on important matters of life and meaning and faith, whose choices I look down on, whose ethics I despise, whose failures I snicker at—they bear the measureless dignity of being formed in the image of almighty God.

And even though I may think myself more moral than my neighbors, more correct about public policy or faith or God than my coworkers, I, too, am infected with the same malady. The same abhorrent instincts live in me. I'm entrapped in the same vast web of deceit, injustice, and foolishness. I'm a fellow miserable offender.

Years ago, I listened to the indie folk artist Sufjan Stevens put this picture of our shared plight in compelling form. My friend Paul invited me to see Stevens in concert at Philadelphia's Academy of Music, and we took in the show together from one of the upper decks in the vast, Gilded Age expanse of that historic concert hall on South Broad Street. Much of the evening was lighthearted, with Stevens and a sizable band careening playfully between the folk, Americana, and electronica that comprise his eclectic musical catalog. I remember there even being a troupe of Hula-Hoop dancers featured in one number.

But when Stevens responded to the chants for an encore from the crowd that packed the sold-out theater, he emerged from the heavy stage drapery alone, the acoustic guitar whose neck he gripped in one hand his only companion for the final act of the performance.

He finished the concert in near-total darkness, standing alone on stage, singing a haunting tune from his album *Illinois*. His closing number was titled "John Wayne Gacy, Jr." after the infamous Chicago-area serial killer and sex offender notorious for hiding twenty-nine of his victims in his suburban ranch-style home, many in the crawl space. The first verses were a sorrowful meditation on Gacy's unspeakable acts. But then

Stevens, in barely a whisper, voiced the final verse of "John Wayne Gacy, Jr." a cappella:

I am really just like him
Look beneath the floorboards
For the secrets I have hid[22]

This is, in a line, the sober prognosis that Christian teaching makes of us: We're not all John Wayne Gacy Jr.—but we've all got some darkness under our floorboards.

HELP

This can seem a morose outlook on life. But when you step back and fix your gaze on the entire canvas of Christian teaching, a much different picture comes into dazzling relief. When we take in the capacious dimensions of the whole Christian narrative, here's what we realize: Christians take an unflinching look in the mirror at our own sin not because we're fixated on bad news but because we're tenacious about good news. Christians articulate a large view of sin because we have a large view of creation—the vast and intricate beauty of the living world, the hallowed goodness of life itself, and the sacred, measureless dignity of every human being. And Christians listen to the unflinching honesty of the Bible's teaching about sin because we have an expansive view of redemption—of the dogged, stubborn work of God to rescue his good creation and of the power, love, and divine resourcefulness at work in our disfigured world to make all things new. Christians believe that God is determined to heal and transfigure the marred state of the world as "far as the curse is found," as the Christmas hymn puts it.[23] Christianity diagnoses our "error bred in the bone"[24] in order to open us to healing, well-being, newness.

My brother Jeremiah's transformation is a picture of this dynamic. Five years my younger, he and our brother, Joel, the middle between us, have been close since we were young. Our whole world shattered to pieces in May 2000 as our parents circled us together in our living room to inform us that my mother had just been diagnosed with an aggressive, advanced-stage strain of colon cancer. Almost exactly a year after they sat us down to break that news, we laid her down into the earth in a graveside service in the little Pennsylvania town where her and our Dad had once met, grown up, and fallen in love. Her sudden absence opened up a dark ache in us all, and Jeremiah, then only a middle-school student, wound up trying to medicate that empty blackness with a narcotics addiction that swallowed up his life.

Jeremiah's life spiraled downward for several years as his addiction slowly strangled the life right out of him. You'd never know it, though, if you met him today. Miah, as we mostly call him, beams a wide smile; he's full of life now. He runs a couple of businesses, has been happily married for years, and is both one of my kids' favorite uncles and one of my best friends. Once, as we were reflecting together on his journey through addiction and recovery, I asked him what his turning point was.

"Oh, that's easy," he replied. He went on to tell me of a night on which he'd overdosed. He had "gone blue"—he was unconscious, his heart was stopping, his skin went pale and cold. Several of the people he had been using with that night panicked, so they dragged his body into the back of a car, rolled him out of the trunk, left him dumped on the pavement outside an ER entrance at a local hospital, and sped away. That night, somehow, he didn't die, and doctors were able to revive him.

"I laid there that night and realized, *I need help, or I'm gonna die.*"

That was the beginning of his recovery. Awareness of his looming death was what ultimately gave him new life. Coming to terms with the ugliness of his sickness was his first step toward health.

This is why the Christian story diagnoses us as miserable offenders—so that we'll look in the mirror, say to ourselves, *I need help, or I'm gonna die*, and then experience the good news that Help has come.

REFLECTION QUESTIONS

1. What do you associate with the concept of sin?

2. How does this chapter change how you think about the human predicament?

3. How do you think recognizing the human predicament might actually be helpful to you?

CHAPTER FIVE
GOD INCARNO
What If God Were One of Us?

Indeed the mystery of Christ runs the risk of being disbelieved precisely because it is so incredibly wonderful. For God was in humanity. He who was above all creation was in our human condition; the invisible one was made visible in the flesh.

CYRIL

That [a force of Love and Logic in the universe] would seek to explain itself is amazing enough. That it would seek to explain itself and describe itself by becoming a child born in straw poverty, in [dung] and straw . . . a child. . . . Just the poetry. . . . Unknowable love, unknowable power, describes itself as the most vulnerable.

BONO

Reza Aslan, a scholar of religion and prominent public intellectual, once sat down for an interview with British comedian John Oliver to promote a provocative biography of Jesus of Nazareth he'd just published entitled *Zealot*. As soon as the segment began, Oliver began to needle Aslan about his book: "Reza, why did you write a book about Jesus? Doesn't everybody know about Jesus at this point? Pretty much everyone in the world now has a relationship with Jesus, whether they want one or not!"[1]

He's right.

Jesus is inescapable. The late Jaroslav Pelikan, an eminent Yale historian, writes that "regardless of what anyone may personally think or believe about him, Jesus of Nazareth has been the dominant figure in the history of Western culture for [more than] twenty centuries. If it were possible, with some sort of super magnet, to pull up out of that history every scrap of metal bearing at least a trace of his name, how much would be left?"[2] Roughly a third of the world's population calls him Lord, prays to him, claims to follow him in some way. Most of the planet marks time by the occasion of his life. Even for the most indifferent, skeptical, or hostile to the faith, the influence of Jesus is inescapable[3]—much that we value about twenty-first-century life, from forgiveness as a moral idea to hospitals, gender equality, universal human rights, and more, would not exist without the influence of Jesus and the movement he started.

But Jesus is both unavoidable and elusive. Here's how biblical scholar N. T. Wright puts this paradox:

> Jesus is unavoidable.
>
> But Jesus is also deeply mysterious. This isn't just because, like any figure of ancient history, we don't know as much about him as we might like. (In fact, we know more about him than we do about most other people from the ancient world. . . .) Jesus is mysterious because what we *do* know—what our evidence encourages us to see as the core of who he was and what he did—is so unlike what we know about anybody else that we are forced to ask, as people evidently did at the time: who, then, *is* this? Who does he think he is, and who is he in fact?[4]

Who is this unavoidable enigma?

IN SEARCH OF AN ENDING

As we discussed in our conversation about God, to uncover who Jesus was and is, we need to acquaint ourselves with the "family story" that he inhabits: that of the first-century Jewish people. The sprawling drama contained in the Hebrew Bible, through which Jesus would see himself and his vocation, functions like "a story in search of an ending."[5] There are scores of narrative threads, winding around, in, and through one another in the Jewish Scriptures, that bear this out.[6]

In Genesis, God creates the human community to bear his image and steward his blessing to the whole creation. As we've explored, we turn away from our Creator, and in that tragic act, this good creation—and every facet of life in it—is disfigured, spoiled. God eventually calls one man—Abraham, whom we've already met, and promises that he'll work through this man's family to rescue the whole of humanity and repair his good, but now very broken, world. There's just one issue though: The people who are supposed to be the solution through which God is going to rescue the world are very much part of the problem. Even a cursory reading of the Jewish Scriptures finds more or less *all* the prominent figures mistrusting God, lying to each other, abusing the poor and vulnerable, and spilling one another's blood, just like all of us do. Is there any such thing as a faithful human being who will carry out the Creator's good purposes for the world?

At the outset of the human story, the Maker shapes a good place for people to put down their roots—Eden—where they are to live together in harmony with one another and their God. Following the primal rebellion, humanity enters a life of exile. This predicament would strike a deep chord with the Jewish people of Jesus' time. Their self-understanding is shaped by the Exodus story—that God heard the pleadings of a tribe of enslaved nobodies, rolled up the divine sleeves in pity and power, and emancipated them into a new life. And along the way, God promised that he'd bring them into a good land—like a new Eden—that would be a place they could call home. God brings them into this land, but soon enough, the old cycles repeat themselves. People turn their backs on God, take advantage of one another, and find themselves in exile. By Jesus' time, they've made it back to their land again but are still enslaved, politically and otherwise. How will they ever get back Home?

The center of the universe for the Jewish people is the Temple. Built in a way intentionally representative of the Genesis depiction of that good cosmos, it is where heaven (God's dimension of reality) and earth (our visible, material dimension) overlap with one another.[7] The Temple wasn't supposed to be an escape from the world, as in other cultic traditions, but a bridgehead reminding the faithful of God's presence and that God promised one day he'd reclaim this broken world. But by the first century, the Temple standing in the heart of Jerusalem has become a sham, built by a Roman governor to keep the locals in line. Will the Temple and its worship ever be restored? And how can people experience the blazingly personal presence of God, anyway?

One of the most fascinating figures in the Scriptures is King David—fiercely trusting of God, fearless in battle, just and fair, and deeply flawed. God made lavish promises of faithfulness to David and his family.[8] And so as subsequent generations of

Israelites are beaten up, pushed around, and carted back and forth from foreign oppressors one after another, they hang on for dear life to the promise that God will raise up another king, a greater Son of great old David, a King who will set things right and rule with the kind of wisdom and justice that will make the trees and hills themselves ring with joy.

The whole Edenic life we were created for—union with God, connection with each other, a true Home in the world—is plunged into ruin when our ancestors listen to the seductive voice of the serpent, that dark, primeval symbol of evil and the Accuser. In response to this, God decrees to the serpent:

> "I will put enmity between you and the woman,
>   and between your offspring and hers;
> he will strike your head,
>   and you will strike his heel."[9]

The Creator decrees a day when a Son of the woman, who will himself be struck in some way by evil, will in so doing crush it underfoot. The Hebrew prophets wait on tiptoe, looking toward that future day when the living One will fashion a new creation out of our old, death-addled one, undoing our mortality itself and regathering a global family together forever. Isaiah, for example, trumpets this future:

> I am about to create new heavens
>   and a new earth;
> the former things shall not be remembered
>   or come to mind. . . .

> The wolf and the lamb shall feed together,
>   the lion shall eat straw like the ox;
>   but the serpent—its food shall be dust!
> They shall not hurt or destroy
>   on all my holy mountain,
>   says the Lord.[10]

Will that future ever arrive in the present? And what child, born of a woman, could possibly reckon with evil once and for all?

Jesus of Nazareth acts and speaks as if *he* is the climax that all those threads (and many others) have been pointing to all along.

I'll never forget watching the movie *The Sixth Sense* for the first time. The psychological thriller follows Dr. Malcolm Crowe, a child psychologist, as he struggles to treat a troubled boy named Cole. The boy insists that he can see ghosts walking around. In the movie's iconic scene, doe-eyed Cole looks at Malcolm and says, in an earnest whisper, "I see dead people."

As the camera pans to Malcolm, he asks, "In your dreams?"

Cole shakes his head.

"While you're awake?"

Cole nods.

"Dead people, like in graves? In coffins?"

Cole shakes his head. "Walking around like regular people. They don't see each other. They only see what they wanna see. They don't know they're dead."[11]

In the moving moments of the film's finale . . .

(Reader, be warned: If you have never seen The Sixth Sense, *I am about to share the piece of information that will totally spoil this movie for you. Although, in fairness, as of this writing, it's been*

released for about twenty-five years, so you've had your chance to see it. Put this book down now and go watch, if you wish, before reading any further. You've been warned. And now, without further ado, here goes . . .)

. . . you discover that Malcolm is, in fact, dead. He's been dead the whole time. All along. When I watched that moment for the first time, I jumped from the couch and yelled at the TV: "WHAT?!?! HOW DID I NOT SEE THAT COMING?!" And what did I do next? I hit Rewind, I watched the whole movie again with that plot twist in mind, and it changed how I encountered every turn in the story.

This is the way the arrival of Jesus works in the larger tapestry of Israel's Scriptures. He's the twist in the plot no one sees coming, the resolution of the Story we've always needed and never would have asked for on our own. And having been surprised by Jesus, the whole Story makes deep, counterintuitive sense in a way we'd never otherwise anticipate.

Jesus, Christians believe, is the True Human Being, who listens faithfully to the voice of the One called Father in a garden at the cost of his life in order to undo our refusal, in the Genesis Garden, to listen to the voice of the One who gave us life. Jesus is God's own self becoming homeless to bring us back Home. Jesus is the Temple in person, the Reality to which the stones and curtains and rituals of the Jerusalem Temple have always pointed; he's our way back into the presence of the One we're made for. Jesus is great David's greater Son, the true King who brings justice to the world even as he endures the worst of our injustice. Jesus is the long-promised Child of a woman, who absorbs the sting of evil to overcome it, who dies for us to live.

GOD WITH US

In Matthew's account of Jesus' beginnings, Jesus' earthly father, Joseph, struggling to reconcile the facts of a fiancée who is both pregnant and swearing her fidelity to him, has a dream in which an angel announces the identity of Mary's mystery Child. Mary's miraculous pregnancy, Matthew tells us, "took place to fulfill what had been spoken by the Lord through the prophet":

> "Look, the virgin shall conceive and bear a son,
>   and they shall name him Emmanuel,"

which means, "God is with us."[12]

This is one of the central mysteries of Christian teaching: We believe that this Child, born under questionable circumstances to two unwed teenagers in a feed trough behind a two-star motel—this Child, who would grow to become a controversial rabbi who shared tables with whores and rubbed it in the noses of every respectable religious leader of his day—is, in fact, God.

The theological term we employ as a shorthand way to name this mystery is *incarnation*. Our English word finds its roots in the Latin word *incarno*, which translates "in flesh/meat." When it's a blustery day and I want to eat something to warm my bones, I'll stop in at Waterway Cafe and ask the waiter for a bowl of chili con carne. When I do so, what I'm requesting is "chili with meat." Christians claim that the human being Jesus of Nazareth is, at the risk of putting it crudely, "God in meat."

The dazzling mystery of the Incarnation means that almighty God became a mortal man. That the Maker stooped to become what had been made. That the invisible One saw fit to show us his face and speak to us in a specific regional dialect, with a particular voice and a local accent. That the Almighty was willing to enter the futilities and fragility of human life. That the King of the universe would live as a powerless Middle Eastern refugee, suffer injustice, and be bound as a prisoner. That the immaterial One would bleed. That Life would die.

> **The dazzling mystery of the Incarnation means that almighty God became a mortal man. That the Maker stooped to become what had been made.**

Thoughtful followers of Jesus have been amazed by this for millennia. The Egyptian church father Cyril of Alexandria wondered poetically at the paradox that Christ is both divine and human:

> Indeed the mystery of Christ runs the risk of being disbelieved precisely because it is so incredibly wonderful. For God was in humanity. He who was above all creation was in our human condition; the invisible one was made visible in the flesh; he who is from the heavens and from on high was in the likeness of earthly things; the immaterial one could be touched; he who is free in his own nature came in the form of a slave; he who blesses all creation became accursed; he who is all righteousness was numbered among transgressors; life itself came in the appearance of death.[13]

We Christians don't believe that God is just some intellectual idea, a vague spiritual force, or a far-off hypothetical construct. We believe that the One who is beyond us has lowered himself to be with us, come among us, and be one of us.

This facet of our faith holds a powerful allure. Bono, lead singer of the rock band U2, in an interview, describes the way in which the Incarnation is at the center of his spiritual beliefs:

> That [a force of Love and Logic in the universe] would seek to explain itself is amazing enough. That it would seek to explain itself and describe itself by becoming a child born in straw poverty, in [dung] and straw . . . a child. . . . Just the poetry. . . . Unknowable love, unknowable power, describes itself as the most vulnerable.[14]

Taking a cue from Bono, this is what we might call the poetry, or music, of the Incarnation. And it's why the truest ways to express this central Christian teaching aren't propositions but music and poetry, symbols and reverence and silence.

A GOD WITH SCARS

I'm often asked by thoughtful friends who are skeptical of Christianity how I could believe in God given the horrors of the world. How on earth could a God worth believing in explain the Holocaust, the Rohingya genocide, or the COVID-19 pandemic?

I don't have all the answers.

On the one hand, many people experience or read about the

cruelties we inflict upon one another, or have inflicted upon us by merciless Mother Nature, and conclude that there must not be a good God out there. I understand this choice, though for me it raises more quandaries than it solves.

On the other, many religious and spiritual traditions have sought to address this in different ways. Many spiritualities claim that God, or the divine, feels compassion for the pain of the world. But here's where Christianity dares what no one else does. Only the Christian gospel claims that, to mend the world God made, God enters it and experiences its very worst. Christians, then, don't claim to know why every terrible thing happens. But we do uniquely believe that the God of the universe has actually experienced the worst of life from the inside. So even though we can't know why we suffer heartbreak, pain, tears, tragedy, and death, we can know that we are never alone in them.

The book of Hebrews, in the New Testament, discusses this dynamic by describing Jesus as humanity's High Priest. In most traditions, a priest is someone who stands between people and God (or the gods) and speaks to one for the other. Jesus, being both fully God and fully human, Hebrews says, is our once-for-all Priest. The author writes that "we do not have a high priest who is unable to sympathize with our weaknesses, but we have one who in every respect has been tested as we are, yet without sin."[15] In Jesus, God knows what human pain, weakness, exhaustion, sorrow, and suffering are. In fact, when you comprehend the immensity of the humiliation the Creator underwent in experiencing a solitary human life, you realize that *all* of Jesus' life was suffering, not just the end of it. Theologian John Calvin, in his writings on the life of Christ, observes that "his whole life was nothing else than a kind of perpetual cross."[16] The shadow of Golgotha loomed all the way back through Jesus' life, right to the manger. All the life he experienced for us was a cross—from the first day to the last.

London pastor and global church leader John Stott wrote that he could only be a Christian because of God's entrance into our suffering, preeminently at the Cross:

> I could never myself believe in God, if it were not for the cross. The only God I believe in is the One Nietzsche ridiculed as "God on the cross." In the real world of pain, how could one worship a God who was immune to it? I have entered many Buddhist temples in different Asian countries and stood respectfully before the statue of the Buddha, his legs crossed, arms folded, eyes closed, the ghost of a smile playing round his mouth, a remote look on his face, detached from the agonies of the world. But each time after a while I have had to turn away. And in imagination I have turned instead to that lonely, twisted, tortured figure on the cross, nails through hands and feet, back lacerated, limbs wrenched, brow bleeding from thorn-pricks, mouth dry and intolerably thirsty, plunged in God-forsaken darkness. That is the God for me! He laid aside his immunity to pain. He entered our world of flesh and blood, tears and death. He suffered for us. Our sufferings become more manageable in the light of his. There is still a question mark against human suffering, but over it we boldly stamp another mark,

the cross that symbolizes divine suffering. "The cross of Christ . . . is God's only self-justification in such a world" as ours.[17]

The only God who makes sense in a world like this? God on the cross.

In my early years as a pastor, I got to know a student I'll call Sonya. Sonya, when my wife and I met her, was a high school sophomore; she was quiet, observant, intelligent. She was an honors student and loved by her friends. But as we got to know her, we realized that her life outside school and church was hell.

Sonya's father had attempted suicide on multiple occasions, and eventually he did end his own life. Her father's death plunged Sonya, understandably, into a deep, black grief. My wife and I spent the next months accompanying her, as best we could, through her journey of loss and sorrow and confusion and anger. We tried to listen, open our home and our lives to her, and be around as much as possible. And over time, Sonya made it through. Her friends loved her. She got wise, caring help. And we sought to be a faithful pastoral presence to her as best we could.

I'll never forget once asking Sonya, as she was beginning to emerge from the fog of grief, about how it was that she still considered herself a Christian.

"Sonya, I've seen people walk away from the faith over a lot less than what you've gone through. How are you still a Christian?"

"Well," she began, "there have been a few things. Friends

have been a lifeline. Counseling has helped. Learning to pray from the Psalms, to express the sadness and anger—that's helped too. And . . ." she trailed off, looking past me.

"What else?" I pressed.

"Well," she continued, "I noticed something else, too. I've been reading the stories of Jesus' crucifixion and resurrection in the Gospels, and I noticed something."

"What's that?"

"What I noticed was that, even after Jesus rose from the dead and all that, when he appeared to the disciples, he still had the scars. He still had the marks of going through all the pain and death."

"That's true, he did," I agreed, not sure where she was going.

"When I realized that, I thought to myself, *Sonya, you can trust a God with scars.*"

This, really, is what the Incarnation means: You can trust a God with scars.

REFLECTION QUESTIONS

1. What, if any, impressions do you have about who Jesus is or what he taught and did?

2. What, in your own words, do you think Christians mean when we talk about "the Incarnation"?

3. What are some of the real-life implications of the Incarnation?

CHAPTER SIX
A CRUCIFIX IN A BAR
Why the Cross Is Good News

> *You can't conceive, my child, nor can I or anyone the ... appalling ... strangeness of the mercy of God.*
>
> Priest in **GRAHAM GREENE**, *Brighton Rock*

> *Jesus' blood never failed me yet*
> *Never failed me yet*
> *Jesus' blood never failed me yet*
> *That's one thing I know*
> *For he loves me so*
>
> **GAVIN BRYARS**, "Jesus' Blood Never Failed Me Yet"

In one episode of the long-running, irreverent sitcom *It's Always Sunny in Philadelphia*, Charlie, Frank, Mac, and Dennis are having a "managerial meeting" at Paddy's, their fictitious Philly bar. As they haggle through the items on their list, they come to one that reads, "a crucifix in the bar." Mac wonders: "Why *wouldn't* we have a crucifix in the bar?"

Charlie counters: "'Cause we're a bar."

"Right," Mac presses, "but we're an *Irish Catholic* bar."

Arguments then ensue over the size and placement of the crucifix, how much blood it will portray, and so on. They eventually compromise and agree that they'll hang a crucifix on the wall in Paddy's, but only in the back, and that they'll only display a "tasteful crucifix."[1]

A "tasteful" cross. In the world in which Jesus lived, that was a contradiction in terms.

Today, the cross has become the most widely known symbol in the world. It features in some of the most enduring art and architecture in Western history. Even if you're completely unfamiliar with the faith, you probably recognize the shape and form of the Christian icon. Crosses stand atop steeples and adorn buildings. The cross turns up everywhere in pop culture, too: on an album cover here, sewn onto a jacket as a fashion statement there. Where I live in South Florida, every year untold numbers of crosses are tattooed onto the collegiate flesh of sunburned spring breakers.

Ironically, in the world from which the Christian movement sprung, the cross was universally recognized too—but no one ever saw a cross and thought or felt anything religious, or tasteful, or fashionable. In Jesus' world, crucifixion was the Roman Empire's most brutal method of execution. Everyone in his time would have known what crucifixions looked like, sounded like, smelled like. The Romans reserved death by crucifixion for slaves, the worst criminals, and those deemed enemies of the state. Victims were crucified nude, in public, as a way for the empire to terrorize its conquered subjects into continued submission. The cross, in short, was scandalous.

Strangely enough, there was a movement that spread across the globe, beginning in the first century AD, that proclaimed that a particular condemned, degraded, crucified person was the true King and Savior of the world—and that this was good news for everyone everywhere.

CRUCIFIED KING

For most residents of the first-century world, what was strange—or downright offensive—about Christian teaching was *not* the idea that a human being might, in some way, be divine or identified with a god. A few decades before Jesus' birth, the Roman general Julius Caesar, having vanquished his foes foreign and domestic, took control of the Roman Republic and ruled as an emperor until he was assassinated. Upon his death, his propagandists claimed that his spirit ascended into heaven from his funeral pyre, and he was proclaimed to have become a god. His adoptive son, Augustus, then ruled the empire for the next four decades; being the son of Julius, he was called divi filius, "son of a god."

Tom Holland, an award-winning historian of antiquity, wrote a compelling book titled *Dominion*, which explores the myriad ways that Christianity has shaped the modern world. In it, he notes this strange feature at the heart of the Christian message:

> Divinity . . . was for the very greatest of the great: for victors, and heroes, and kings. Its measure was the power to torture one's enemies, not to suffer it oneself: to nail them to the rocks of a mountain, or to turn them into spiders, or to blind and crucify them after conquering the world. That a man who had himself been crucified might be hailed as a god could not help but be seen by people everywhere across the Roman world as scandalous, obscene, grotesque.[2]

It wasn't, then, just the proclamation that a human being was divine that made Christianity a scandal throughout the world. It was the proclamation that Jesus of Nazareth, *who had been condemned and crucified*, was the world's true Lord and God.

If things like branding consultants and marketing teams existed in the first century, they'd certainly have advised the early Christians to minimize or eliminate Jesus' crucifixion from their messaging. But even a brief look at the early Christian movement reveals that they did exactly the opposite. The cross, offensive as it was, was at the very heart of the Christian faith from its very beginning.

This comes through, for example, in the shape of the Gospel accounts of Jesus' teaching and life. Think of the last time you read a biography or watched a documentary about someone famous or noteworthy: Nelson Mandela or JFK or Tupac Shakur. Even if the circumstances or events of their death were mysterious or nefarious, ordinarily, documenting someone's end takes up only a small amount of the pages or screen minutes devoted to narrating the whole of their life.

No so when it comes to Jesus. He was executed at thirty-three years old. But in the fourth Gospel, for example, John takes eleven chapters to unfold what he wants us to know of Jesus' entire life and then a full ten chapters to narrate his final week, his sufferings and death, and his resurrection. And the same dynamic holds true in the other three Gospels included in the Christian Scriptures. Read the Gospel of Mark, for example. It's the shortest of the four Gospels, and most scholars believe it was the first one written down and circulated to young church communities. Mark takes ten chapters to tell us about Jesus' life, teaching, miracles, and the movement he led (and includes nothing about Jesus' birth or childhood) and then takes the whole final third of the book to recount Jesus' final week. In fact, nineteenth-century scholar Martin Kähler called the Gospel of Mark "a passion narrative with an extended introduction."[3]

The cross was the brand of the Christian church from her very earliest days. In fact, the cross was so closely associated with Christians that they were often ridiculed for it. The earliest pictorial description archaeologists have recovered of Jesus of Nazareth comes from a drawing scratched into plaster at the Palatine Hill in Rome. Scrawled into that wall originally to mock someone named Alexamenos, the drawing depicts him worshiping a person with the torso and lower body of a man and the head of a donkey on a cross. Beneath the drawing, an inscription in Greek reads, "Alexamenos worshipping his god."[4]

WHAT'S THE DEAL WITH THE CROSS?

In my early years as a church planter, I once participated in a Q&A panel at a local university to interact with students' questions about faith and spirituality. We had a number of fascinating conversations that evening. But I'll never forget one particular student, sitting attentively in the back of the auditorium, wiping his tangle of curly hair away from his eyes every so often to scribble some notes into a notebook. Near the end of the event, his hand shot up. "What is the whole deal," he asked, "with the cross?"

"Could you share a little more of what you're wondering about?" I asked.

"Well, you see lots of crosses in churches and on Christian buildings and stuff. And Jesus is always on the cross in Christian artwork. Why is he always pictured on a cross? Why is that so important?"

I told him that he, knowingly or not, was asking one of the most central questions of the Christian faith.

So what's the deal with the cross?

One popular approach to Jesus, for some time now, has been to treat his death as a tragic turn of events—to see his demise on a Roman cross as the unfortunate end to the life of someone who was really just a noble mystic or a misunderstood political zealot. There are several problems with this approach, however. One is that if Jesus were merely a wise man or a revolutionary whose life was violently snuffed out by the Romans, there's virtually no chance that we'd have ever heard of him. In an op-ed reviewing a book advocating one such portrait of Jesus, *New York Times* columnist Ross Douthat makes just this point:

> There's enough gospel material to make . . . these portraits credible. But they also tend to be rather, well, boring, and to raise the question of how a pedestrian figure—one zealot among many, one mystic in a Mediterranean full of them—inspired a global faith.[5]

Jesus of Nazareth, in other words, is hardly the only would-be revolutionary or wise man the Romans crucified; they crucified untold thousands of people. So if Jesus were really nothing more than that, we'd know about as much about him as we do all those other lives the Roman state efficiently snuffed out (which is to say, little to nothing).

This also isn't how the very first Christians themselves—the ones who would have personally known, listened to, and followed Jesus—saw the death of their Teacher and Lord. One of the very earliest formulations of Christian teaching is found in a letter written to the church in Corinth. Paul, who writes what we now call 1 Corinthians, quotes it to the community with whom he's corresponding: "I handed on to you as of first importance what I in turn had received: that Christ died for our sins in accordance with the scriptures."[6] The first Christians saw the death of Jesus as no accident, no mere act of meaningless state cruelty. They saw his crucifixion as being "in accordance with the scriptures"; as being, in other words, in concert with the whole long, winding Story of God in the world—and, counterintuitively, where the Story had always been going.

What's more, this isn't how Jesus himself saw his death. If you're intrigued by the teachings of Jesus and want to take him seriously, you've got to interact with the whole of what he says. And so you've got to do business with the fact that the same Jesus who told his followers to live by the Golden Rule, commanded the rich to give their money away, and taught forgiveness and compassion also said things like this:

> "The Son of Man must undergo great suffering, and be rejected by the elders, chief priests, and scribes, and be killed, and on the third day be raised."[7]

> "Let these words sink into your ears: The Son of Man is going to be betrayed into human hands."[8]

> "See, we are going up to Jerusalem, and everything that is written about the Son of Man by the prophets will be accomplished. For he will be handed over to the

Gentiles; and he will be mocked and insulted and spat upon. After they have flogged him, they will kill him, and on the third day he will rise again."[9]

Listen to the resolve in Jesus' voice: The Son of Man *must* suffer. Everything written *will be* accomplished. The events of Jesus' suffering and death aren't accidental; they're shot through with God's determined resolve to reclaim and renew a fractured creation.

So: What's the deal with the cross? Why did Jesus die?

At one level, it's not a hard question to answer. Jesus died because someone in his inner circle sold him out for some cash. Jesus died because he infuriated the religious establishment of his day. Jesus died because he said and did things that suggested he was a king and the Roman Empire did not take kindly to would-be kings.

These are the circumstantial reasons Jesus died. But they're not the deepest responses to the question. Here's a different way of asking it: *What was God doing through the death of Jesus?*

One of the central Christian creeds, developed a few centuries later, articulates that all that Jesus did, and all that was done to him, is "for us and for our salvation."[10] So, essentially, Jesus' death was *for us* and *for our sin*.

Here's yet another way of asking it: *What is God doing for us through the death of Jesus?* Christians have reached to find language adequate to describe this bottomless mystery for millennia now. The explanations that the church has developed for what transpired in the cosmos as Jesus endured the Cross are sometimes called atonement theories, and Christian thinkers have developed a variety of them—all of them admittedly only partially adequate to give human expression to a measureless wonder. Each of them, in analogy and poetry, image and song, portrays the cosmic and many-sided effects of Jesus' death.[11] Here are a few of the main ones.[12]

Rescue

The dramatic story of the Exodus is one of the most well known in the world. The living God hears the pained cries of the Hebrew people, who are, at the time, a tribe of nobodies, languishing in slavery under the thumb of the Egyptian pharaoh. God rolls up his divine sleeves and emancipates them in breathtaking fashion. He parts the Red Sea, bringing them through certain death to the other side and into a new life as his own family. The Exodus story came to be the defining narrative for the people of Israel; it shaped how they saw themselves and how they understood God. The theme of deliverance or salvation becomes prominent in the Exodus story, and it became a rich, central concept in Jewish life. It appears throughout the Old Testament, and the Old Testament writers often refer back to this central event of deliverance. This, fundamentally, is what God does: looses, delivers, saves.[13]

It's no accident that Jesus was crucified at the Passover Festival—the annual festival in which the Jewish people would rehearse the Exodus story and remember their freedom and identity. By the first century, the Israelites were looking for God to do an Exodus again—to free them from Rome's tyrannical clutches. We know that there were frequent uprisings around Passover time in Jerusalem.

As Jesus traveled with his followers to Jerusalem, he spoke knowingly of the death that awaited him there. On one occasion, Jesus speaks specifically of his looming "departure" (as many translations render it).[14] When we read that sentence in English, it's easy to assume that "departure" is just a euphemism for Jesus' death. But the word Luke uses is actually the Greek word for "exodus." In other words, Luke wants us to see, as we travel with Jesus to Jerusalem, that the events that transpire there—Jesus' suffering, death, and resurrection—will be like a new Exodus. At the Cross, God is accomplishing an exodus—not just to free one group of people from sociopolitical oppression at the hands of the empire du jour but to liberate the whole world from our older, darker foes: sin and death. Jesus' death rescues us from death and looses us into new life.

Victory

A victorious Roman military general upon returning to Rome after having vanquished his enemies would often have a lavish military parade called a triumph thrown for him. There'd be laurels, adoring crowds throwing flowers, marching troops, and, of course, a parade of captured foes—sometimes including the conquered enemy king—on their way to crucifixion and death.[15]

In a wry irony, the New Testament uses this very imagery to describe the cosmic events that transpired at the Cross of Christ:

> [God] forgave us all our trespasses, erasing the record that stood against us with its legal demands. He set this aside, nailing it to the cross. He disarmed the rulers and authorities and made a public example of them, triumphing over them in it.[16]

It's through a cross—that ultimate symbol of defeat and shame—that God, through Christ, parades in cosmic triumph. God wins the ultimate victory over the evil oppressing us and the universe by absorbing the worst of it. God defeats our violence and injustice by suffering our violence and injustice. At the death of Jesus, God once and for all puts the power of death to death.

This ironic inversion turns up everywhere in the Christian Scriptures. The Gospel of Matthew, for example, narrates Jesus' trial, suffering, and death like an enthronement ceremony, with Jesus repeatedly being called "King of the Jews"[17]—but not at the head of an army or in the throne room of a palace. Jesus is lauded as King as he's mocked, tortured, and executed. This, Matthew announces, is what the world's true King is like: He loves us enough to be nailed to his throne.

The final word in the Bible, the Revelation to John, repeats this refrain too. John's wild, apocalyptic visions of heaven (God's dimension of reality) picture all the cosmos celebrating the victorious God; but God is identified together with a Lamb, sacrificially slain, and it's through the Lamb's sacrifice that God wins the ultimate cosmic victory over evil and death.[18]

Sacrifice

As you read your way through the Bible, you'll discover quite a lot of material related to sacrifices. The imagery of sacrifice is foreign to most of us in the twenty-first century, but it constituted a significant part of Jewish worship, and there's a whole book in the Hebrew Bible (Leviticus) full of rich reflection on sacrifice. In Jewish practice, you'd offer a sacrifice to redeem, or buy back, your firstborn son as a way to remember that all life is a gift from God. You'd offer sacrifices in thanks to God for the year's harvest. You'd sacrifice to demonstrate God's forgiveness, which does away with guilt and reunites humanity and God in peace. It's no surprise, then, that this is one main way the early Christians talked about the death of Jesus: The shedding of his blood was the sacrifice to end all sacrifices, the once-for-all act to make atonement for—that is, to pay for—the sin of the world and open a "new and living way"[19] for us to be reconciled with the God we're made for. Think of the origin of the word *atonement*: It's literally "at-one-ment"; through Jesus' sacrifice, we're reunited with our Creator.

Some ways of articulating this motif are more helpful than others, and at times the way some Christians have expressed this teaching has created the impression that at the Cross there's some sort of cosmic child abuse going on: an angry Father punishing an innocent Son rather than us. But this caricature forgets the Christian teaching of the Trinity: The living God is, in his own being, a unified relationship of love. And so the cross doesn't represent one member of the Trinity taking out divine wrath on another; it represents the living God acting to offer his own self in our place to deal with our sin.[20]

When talking about the story of the Cross, I've often listened to people wonder, "Why does Jesus have to die for God to forgive people? Can't God just choose to forgive?" But anyone who's ever attempted to forgive an unfaithful spouse or the betrayal of a trusted coworker or the failures of a parent implicitly understands the answer to this question—forgiveness is *costly*.

In 1995, South Africa, newly free from a half century of apartheid, established the Truth and Reconciliation Commission to try to heal the divide between white and Black South Africans.

They provided a public space for Black South Africans to name the violence and harm done to them and for white South Africans to receive pardon for racist acts committed. When Desmond Tutu was appointed to head the commission, he released a compelling public statement that articulated honestly the need for the work that faced them, saying, "We cannot be facile and say bygones will be bygones, because they will not be bygones and will return to haunt us. True reconciliation is never cheap, for it is based on forgiveness which is costly."[21] Tutu named what we all know: Real forgiveness is costly. Christ's willing sacrifice displays for us in the starkest way possible the infinitely costly love of God.

> **Christ's willing sacrifice displays for us in the starkest way possible the infinitely costly love of God.**

Revelation

One of the most magnificent poems in the Bible is the soaring first section of the Gospel of John.[22] Its first eighteen verses are multilayered, symphonic: In introducing us to Jesus, John draws together light and darkness, Hebrew Scripture and Greek philosophy, the Creation story and the Exodus events. At the climax of this passage, John trumpets that "the Word became flesh and lived among us, and we have seen his glory, the glory as of a father's only son, full of grace and truth."[23] John wants us to watch the story of Jesus unfold and experience the staggering realization *This is what the invisible God is really like!*

John organizes his Gospel around signs that Jesus performs, which unveil, one after another, just who this mysterious Teacher from Galilee truly is. And just as the Creation poetry of Genesis 1 is organized around seven days of Creation, the Gospel of John is shaped by seven of Jesus' signs. So, for example, in John 2, Jesus creates 180 gallons or so of the very best wine for the wedding of someone who may have been a family friend. And after telling us the story, John adds: "Jesus did this, the first of his signs, in Cana of Galilee, and revealed his glory."[24] He wants us to watch Jesus and realize for ourselves: *The Word became flesh and celebrated a wedding, and we have seen his glory—glory as of the One who lavishes on us the wine of God's joy.*

Two chapters later, Jesus heals a royal official's son . . . *and the Word became flesh and healed a sick boy, and we have seen his glory, the glory as of the One who heals our diseases.*

In John 6, Jesus feeds hungry masses on a desolate Galilean hillside . . . *and the Word became flesh and fed thousands, and we have seen his glory, the glory as of the One who gives food to the hungry.*

All in all, there are six miraculous signs in John 1–11, culminating in Jesus' raising of his friend Lazarus from death. And then, beginning in John 12, we follow Jesus to Jerusalem and ultimately to his death. So what's the final, seventh sign in John's narrative architecture? The Cross.

And the Word became flesh and died among us. And we have seen his glory, the glory as of the One who laid down his life on our behalf.

Ultimately, it's when we look at the bent figure of Jesus of Nazareth, nailed to the rough wood of a Roman execution instrument, mocked by the religious establishment, sneered at by passersby, bleeding and expiring, "for us and for our salvation," that we truly discover, *This is what the God of the universe is really like.*

In my experience, it's often art and poetry that evoke what prosaic explanation simply can't—and that's nowhere truer than when taking in the unfathomable mysteries of Jesus' death. I offer you this meditation by sixteenth-century Welsh poet George Herbert, from his poem "The Agony," as he reflects on the Cross of Jesus that the bread and wine of Holy Communion, which Christians receive in worship to remember Jesus' sacrifice, depict:

> *Who knows not Love, let him assay*
> *And taste that juice which, on the cross, a pike*
> *Did set again abroach; then let him say*
> *If ever he did taste the like,*
> *Love is that liquor sweet and most divine,*
> *Which my God feels as blood, but I as wine.*[25]

REFLECTION QUESTIONS

1. Where have you seen crosses? What do you associate with the image of the cross?

2. Why do you think Jesus' death on a cross is so central to the Christian faith?

3. Which, if any, of the various meanings of the Cross do you resonate with?

CHAPTER SEVEN
NOTHING TO BE FRIGHTENED OF
The Hope of Resurrection

> *Make no mistake: if He rose at all*
> *it was as His body.*
> **JOHN UPDIKE,** "Seven Stanzas at Easter"
>
> *If Christ is risen, nothing else matters.*
> *And if Christ is not risen—nothing else matters.*
> **JAROSLAV PELIKAN**

British writer Julian Barnes begins his memoir *Nothing to Be Frightened Of* by admitting, "I don't believe in God, but I miss Him."[1] Barnes's disbelief is thoroughgoing; his father was an agnostic and his mother an avowed skeptic who told her son in no uncertain terms she didn't want "any of that [religious] mumbo-jumbo" at her funeral.[2] He was never baptized, never joined a church, never professed a faith he went on to lose. But the unavoidable finality of death made him ponder the possibility of God's existence and the afterlife. He calls the Christian story "one of the haunting hypotheticals for the nonbeliever."[3] Barnes takes the title of his autobiography from one of his journal entries from two decades prior: "People say of death,

'There's nothing to be frightened of.' They say it quickly, casually. Now let's say it again, slowly, with re-emphasis. 'There's NOTHING to be frightened of.'" And then, for good measure, he adds a line by French writer Jules Renard: "The word that is most true, most exact, most filled with meaning, is the word 'nothing.'"[4]

There's *nothing* to be frightened of.

In Mark's account of Jesus' resurrection, Mary Magdalene and a couple of her companions trek to Jesus' tomb in the first blinks of daylight to anoint his body with burial spices. They're not decked out in pastel dresses, pearls, or any such holiday finery this morning—Mary and her friends are not en route to an Easter celebration. They're not celebrating anything, in fact. They begin the morning of the first Easter aching with grief. As the tomb comes into view, the pace of their slow shuffle quickens: The stone has been rolled back, and the door is now wide open. Sorrow ebbs at a surge of alarm and then outright terror. As Mark tells it, the body of Jesus is nowhere to be seen, and the person they do see is a messenger from the heavens, dressed in gleaming white.

The angelic figure speaks, gentle and strong (and I think it's best to hear this quintessential sentence of Scripture in the old King James translation):

> Be not affrighted: Ye seek Jesus of Nazareth, which was crucified: he is risen; he is not here: behold the place where they laid him.[5]

Be not affrighted.
Be not afraid.

There's nothing to be frightened of.

You might be interested to know that this is the most often repeated command in the Bible. Not "Thou shalt not commit adultery." Not "Do unto others as you would have them do unto you." Not "Give the church your money."

It is *Do not be afraid.*

In a fearful world, to human beings who have spent millennia terrorizing and being terrorized, to a creation in the clutches of death, the Author of life persistently pronounces, "Be not afraid."

This, then, is the question. It's the question at the very root of the Christian faith. It's the question that sneaks up on everyone, believer and doubter alike, in unguarded, quiet moments, as you walk through a cemetery or read an obituary headed by a familiar name. It's the question that ambushes us all when the test results reveal the worst or we sit beside a parent or a friend or a lover or a child as they expel a last breath from their chest.

Who's right? Julian Barnes? Or Jesus of Nazareth?

Is there waiting for each of us, and the whole cosmos, an inevitable, vast abyss of empty extinction? An unavoidable, yawning, insatiable NOTHING that ought to unnerve the most composed of us? Or can you actually take the daring gospel announcement seriously? Can you responsibly believe in the twenty-first century that, because of what God did in the body of Jesus on the first Easter and the eruption of life and grace let loose into the universe on that day, you can look into the abyss and not be afraid?

Is there NOTHING to be frightened of?

Or, thanks to Jesus, is there actually nothing to be frightened of?

CHRONOLOGICAL SNOBBERY

Allow me to introduce my former neighbor Tom. He used to live one door up from us; he was a university professor possessed of a fast mind and a faster mouth. One of the first times we met after my family moved in, I noticed Tom on his front steps with a bestselling then-new release from a prominent figure in the New Atheism movement. I asked him what he thought of the book, and Tom didn't miss a minute before waxing eloquent on how, in his words, "no one who went to college in the twenty-first century could possibly believe in God or Jesus and all that 'born of a virgin, raised from the dead' stuff"; and, after pausing, he pressed his point home: "Anyone who believes stuff like that is an idiot!"

Here I need to promise you this is not the exaggeration of a preacher; this was the very next sentence to leave his mouth:

"Say, what do you do for a living?"

I smiled and told him, "Well, Tom, I've got some bad news for you. I'm a professional idiot."

Tucked behind my neighbor Tom's seemingly rational pronouncement is what a writer named C. S. Lewis would call "chronological snobbery."[6]

Many people react this way, intentionally or not, when they encounter the astounding story of the Resurrection. "Now that we're in the twenty-first century . . ."; "Now that we have modern science and medicine . . ."; "Now that we're educated . . ."; "Now that we know that an intelligent person couldn't believe the Resurrection actually happened . . ."

This knee-jerk reaction many of us share, though, misses one glaring thing: The Resurrection would have been just as hard to take seriously in the first century as it is in the twenty-first century. To put it simply: People die and stay dead with remarkable consistency. And that's been happening for a long time now.

Christians knew this just as well in the first century as you and I do in the twenty-first. And yet they unblushingly announced the Resurrection as first-order news for the whole world. In one of the earliest letters that wound up becoming part of Christian Scripture, Paul (one of the main first-generation leaders of the Christian movement) quotes a brief summary of Christian teaching that would have been memorized, learned, and passed on from Christianity's earliest embryonic beginnings: "I handed on to you as of first importance what I in turn had received: that Christ died for our sins in accordance with the scriptures, and that he was buried, and that he was raised on the third day in accordance with the scriptures."[7]

Here's what's of first-order importance, says Paul. Christ died—really died. Buried-in-the-ground died. And Christ was raised.

NOTHING ELSE MATTERS

Christians and skeptics agree on this: Christianity stands or falls with the Resurrection. This is the cornerstone of all Christian belief and faith. It's said that among the last words of historian Jaroslav Pelikan were these: "If Christ is risen, nothing else matters. And if Christ is not risen—nothing else matters."

Paul says as much. Later in the same letter, Paul puts it bluntly: "If Christ has not been raised, then our proclamation has been in vain and your faith has been in vain."[8] If Christ isn't risen, the Christian faith unravels like a cheap dress. If Jesus is still in the grave, he's not a great moral teacher or a wise guru—he's a sideshow huckster.

Paul goes on: "If Christ has not been raised, your faith is futile and you are still in your sins. Then those also who have died in Christ have perished. If for this life only we have hoped in Christ, we are of all people most to be pitied."[9]

> **In an act of power and love not seen since the dawn of the cosmos, the Creator raised Jesus into new life, breaking the stranglehold of sin, evil, and death on his good creation and beginning his work of making all things new.**

In other words, if the tomb of Jesus is not empty, then the Christian faith itself is completely empty. The stains soaked deep in my soul of the worst that I've done aren't coming out. If Christ is dead, then it's death that has the last word in the world. Your life and mine, and every human being's, every single creation of beauty and each act of goodness, kindness, and justice in the history of the world—all these are so many meaningless smudges on the windshield of cosmic history. If Christ is not risen: Eat, drink, and self-medicate.

If Christ is not risen, nothing else matters.

But, says Paul, and every believing follower of Jesus: Christ *is* risen. Something has happened, out in the open in world history, that has changed everything, for everyone and everything, forever. And so nothing else matters.

To help you take in just how outlandish the Christian story's central claim is, I want to be clear. When Christians say we believe that, on the first Easter morning, Christ was raised from the dead, we don't mean that Jesus' inspiring example will somehow live on forever. We don't mean that his teachings still speak to us from beyond the grave. When we talk about resurrection, we're not referencing the inspiring refreshment of springtime, or the potential of the human spirit, or the power of optimism.

We mean that the crucified, executed person of Jesus of Nazareth was raised from death by the power and love of God. We mean that Jesus, as it were, "had come *through death and out the other side*" into new, bodily, this-worldly life.[10]

In the 1950s, author John Updike submitted a poem entitled "Seven Stanzas at Easter" to an arts festival. It begins bluntly:

Make no mistake: if He rose at all
it was as His body.[11]

Over the seven verses that follow, Updike unfolds the staggering dimensions of Easter: the belief that, three days after Jesus heaved his final breath, his tortured body was reknit, his expired heart began its beat anew, his life was rekindled. And in an act of power and love not seen since the dawn of the cosmos, the Creator raised Jesus into new life, breaking the stranglehold of sin, evil, and death on his good creation and beginning his work of making all things new.

TESTIMONY

If Christ rose, then nothing else matters. So did he?

Over the years I've had many thoughtful friends wonder the same question: How on earth, against the data of what we see happen to every human life at its conclusion, can someone responsibly believe that Jesus rose from the dead?

In a word: *testimony*. The claims of Jesus' resurrection from the dead are verified by scores and scores of eyewitness testimony. For starters, there are the earliest known reports of the raising of Jesus, which are addressed in a chapter we've already considered, 1 Corinthians 15. After claiming that Jesus has risen from the dead, Paul goes on to relay that "he appeared to Cephas, then to the twelve. Then he appeared to more than five hundred brothers and sisters at one time, most of whom are still alive, though some have died. Then he appeared to James, then to all the apostles."[12]

In citing all these witnesses, it's as if Paul is saying, "I know this sounds crazy—but if you don't believe me, ask around." We know, historically speaking, that this letter was written within a couple of decades of Christianity's beginning, when most of the people named would have still been living, and was widely circulated around the regions where most of them lived. All it would have taken to discredit the early Christians was for one of these supposed witnesses to say, "No, no, this was all a ruse"—and yet this never happened. Scores of the first generations of these witnesses, in fact, wound up being tortured and killed for their testimony of Jesus' resurrection. Now, sadly, lots of people in human history have given their lives for something that turns out to be a lie—but no one dies for something they themselves know is a lie. As Blaise Pascal once said, "I [believe] those witnesses that get their throats cut."[13]

Then there are the Gospel accounts of Jesus' resurrection. Scholars have concluded that they're also based on eyewitness testimony and were written within the first several decades after the first Easter, when many of the people named in them would have still been alive and around to discredit the Gospels' claims if they were false.[14] And the accounts of the Resurrection they contain are written far too counterproductively to reasonably think they're fabrications. The main factor in this regard is the prominence of women in the stories. In each of the four Gospels, it is women who are the first witnesses of the empty tomb and who first meet Jesus. As biblical scholar N. T. Wright observes, women occupied an exceptionally low place in the world of the Roman Empire.[15] The testimony of women was not admissible in court in this culture. So if the Gospel writers were going to make up a story about Jesus rising from the dead and desired it to be believable, they'd never have women be the first eyewitnesses. Wright notes that early opponents often scoffed at Christianity because of this. Furthermore, as we discussed near the beginning of this book, all the male disciples who would wind up becoming the church's first leaders come off very badly. They question or scoff at the Resurrection; they don't recognize Jesus at first. To put it simply, if you were going to make up the Resurrection story, you'd never do it like the Gospels do.

And there's another layer to the puzzle. It's not enough to just say that you don't believe the testimony of the early Christians that Jesus was raised from the dead. If you say that, you also need a more likely explanation for the overnight explosion of the Christian movement across the world. This conundrum has occupied scholars and historians for centuries, and I'm not going to spend a lot of time on the various theories that have developed—but I will say that each of them has proven fatally flawed.[16] I'll mention just a few so you can see what I mean.

Some have claimed that perhaps Jesus didn't actually die on the cross and resuscitated in the tomb. The problem with this is that Jesus was killed by people who were killing experts. A Roman soldier who failed to execute a prisoner condemned to crucifixion would themselves be crucified. And even if Jesus somehow didn't die and did revive in the tomb, he'd be in for a long, slow recovery and would certainly not convince anybody that he was the risen Lord of the world.

Others have proposed that perhaps the first disciples had some kind of group hallucination or experience of cognitive dissonance or that they had a "spiritual experience" of Jesus of some kind. The issue with this idea, however, is that human beings don't have group experiences of this kind. And early Christians had language for having spiritual experiences—and this isn't the language they used to describe their experiences of Jesus. They used the language of bodily resurrection.

As N. T. Wright concludes, "The best explanation by far for the rise of Christianity is that Jesus really did reappear, not as a battered, bleeding survivor, not as a ghost (the stories are very clear about that), but as a living, bodily human being."[17] It explodes our mental circuitry and bursts our brittle boundaries of what we think possible, but here's the best explanation for what happened on that first Easter: *Christ is risen.*

BIG BANG

Church leader Rowan Williams, whose letter to a little girl we read earlier, compares the Resurrection to a "second 'Big Bang'":

"a tumultuous surge of divine energy as fiery and intense as the very beginning of the universe."[18] So what was happening at the empty tomb of Jesus? What was let loose in the cosmos, and in the depths of a human life, as Jesus burst through the grave into new life?

The various writers of the New Testament pile image upon image to find language to describe what Easter means. At times they talk about the Resurrection in terms of a new Exodus, this time to emancipate not just one group of people trapped in sociopolitical slavery but to liberate the whole world from our ancient enemies of evil, darkness, and death.

This Exodus image portrays how a Christian now has a *new identity* if she belongs to Jesus. Several passages in the Scriptures describe how, in a real sense, the Christian dies and rises to a new life together with Jesus. Writing to the church community in the city of Rome, for example, Paul reminds his readers that "all of us who have been baptized into Christ Jesus were baptized into his death . . . we have been buried with him by baptism into death, so that, just as Christ was raised from the dead by the glory of the Father, so we too might walk in newness of life."[19]

For everyone identified with Christ by baptism and faith, then, Jesus' story is now their story. What is most true for a Christian, thanks to Jesus' rising, is not whatever she has done or hasn't done in life. It's not the shame of her past or the uncertainties of her future. It's not her relationship status or socioeconomic status. It's not whatever evil she's inflicted on others or had others inflict on her. It's what Christ Jesus has done for her.

In some places, the Scriptures relate the implications of the Resurrection by means of the agricultural images of seed and harvest. The raising of Christ was like the first fruits, Paul writes in 1 Corinthians 15, of the full harvest of new life that God will bring about in the future.

Other places in the New Testament talk about the events of Easter as a kind of cosmic battle that Christ has now won over all the heavenly and earthly forces of darkness. In the book of Ephesians, for example, Paul trumpets that "God put [his] power to work in Christ when he raised him from the dead and seated him at his right hand in the heavenly places, far above all rule and authority and power and dominion."[20] There's an early Easter prayer that celebrates Easter as a battle won:

Christ is risen from the dead,
trampling down death by death,
and upon those in the tombs bestowing life![21]

One of my favorite depictions of Easter morning captures this motif dramatically. In the iconography (a particular kind of painting used to depict the events of Jesus' life) of Easter in the Eastern Orthodox part of the Christian church, Jesus is often depicted as smashing down the door of the tomb, trampling demons underfoot, and pulling Adam and Eve, representatives of the entire human race under the thumb of death, up from the grave into new life.

These images of the seed and the battle portray the way the Resurrection offers Christians *new hope*. Think with me about what deep sense this makes of how we experience death. Various cultures and worldviews see death in different ways. In the modern, secular narrative of life, death is simply the inevitable, meaningless end to a brief, meaningless existence. Certain religions see death as part of an endless cycle of ending and rebirth. Some Eastern spiritualities see death as an illusion to be overcome.

But in the biblical narrative, death is an intruder, a midnight vandal in the good world God made. Death is a pollutant, a cancer. The New Testament calls death "the last enemy."[22] When you stand beside the casket of a friend or a spouse or a child who's died too young, when you get the phone call relaying your worst fears, when you brush close with sickness and mortality yourself, you know that death isn't an illusion, and it's not just "part of the journey"—it's an *enemy*.

The hope of the Easter gospel is that God has broken the power of the last enemy. That even the grave itself is nothing to be frightened of.

BE NOT PROUD

One of my favorite poets is John Donne, a seventeenth-century English writer and Anglican priest. On one occasion, he had a major bout of illness, which many believe was typhoid fever, that brought him to the doorstep of death. The experience inspired him to write what's become one his most famous sonnets, "Death, Be Not Proud," which expresses the hope of resurrection at the edge of the grave:

> *Death, be not proud, though some have called thee*
> *Mighty and dreadful, for thou art not so:*
> *For those whom thou think'st thou dost overthrow*
> *Die not, poor Death, nor yet canst thou kill me. . . .*
> *Thou art slave to fate, chance, kings, and desperate men,*
> *And dost with poison, war, and sickness dwell . . .*

> *One short sleep past, we wake eternally*
> *And death shall be no more; Death, thou shalt die.*[23]

If the Victorian English is a little hard to follow, this is what Donne knew: In Christ, there's nothing to be frightened of.

REFLECTION QUESTIONS

1. Why do you think the resurrection of Jesus is so important to the Christian faith?

2. Why is it difficult to believe in the Resurrection?

3. What do you think are some of the most compelling reasons for and against believing in the resurrection of Jesus?

4. If Jesus' resurrection were true, what would that mean for you?

CHAPTER EIGHT

I'LL BE THERE IN SPIRIT

Experiencing God's Spirit

> *The dove descending breaks the air*
> *With flame of incandescent terror*
> *Of which the tongues declare*
> *The one discharge from sin and error.*
> *The only hope, or else despair*
> *Lies in the choice of pyre or pyre—*
> *To be redeemed from fire by fire.*
>
> **T. S. ELIOT**, "Little Gidding"

The film *Midnight in Paris* follows the unusual events in the life of Gil, a prosperous Hollywood screenwriter, as he goes on holiday in Paris with his affluent, acquisitive fiancée, Inez.[1] Gil doesn't see an ounce of originality in his work; he'd rather be writing novels than movie scripts. He pines nostalgically for 1920s Paris: If only he could have been there back then! He would have been right at home, he thinks, immersed in a literary scene that included Scott and Zelda Fitzgerald, Ernest Hemingway, Gertrude Stein, E. E. Cummings, and others.

One evening, while Gil is sulking in his own sadness, the clock strikes midnight, and suddenly—magically!—he is transported back to the 1920s of his dreams. He gets to rub shoulders with all the Lost Generation greats back in "the good old days." And he's smitten with a costume designer he meets named Adriana. They bond over nostalgia—except, in a cruel twist, the past she loves is the 1890s and not her distasteful present. His Lost Generation dream woman hates being in the Lost Generation.

Many people experience the same sort of nostalgia as they consider Jesus of Nazareth. Curious and committed alike are captivated by his teachings, entranced by the stories of his miracles and healings, puzzled and provoked by the announcement of his resurrection. It'd be marvelous if what we read on the page were true, but can we really know for sure? And so we sigh and say, *If only I had been there back then!*

IF ONLY I HAD BEEN THERE

Here's the irony. The four Gospels themselves don't see it that way. On the one hand, in his lifetime, Jesus' family and closest friends often misunderstood him. One of them denied him in his most dire hour, and another betrayed him. Many people who met or interacted with Jesus found him compelling, but many others found him puzzling, infuriating, or downright insane.

On the other, Jesus promised to remain personally present to his company of followers beyond his death and resurrection—but in a different fashion that would still somehow be every bit as real. Standing at the precipice of his suffering and death, Jesus offered a final word to his disciples—a symphonic, multi-layered piece of teaching and praying found in John 14 to 16. In it, he warns soberly of his imminent departure but promises that his approaching absence will be accompanied by a new sort of presence. This interplay between presence and absence is woven throughout Jesus' final instructions and prayer for his apprentices; in these three chapters, Jesus says he's about to go away some fifteen times and promises that his Spirit, or God's Spirit, or God, is about to come to them some twenty-six times.

"I will ask the Father," Jesus promises his friends, "and he will give you another Advocate, to be with you forever. This is the Spirit of truth. . . . I will not leave you orphaned; I am coming to you."[2] Jesus even goes so far as to say that this arrangement will be better for his followers: "I tell you the truth: it is to your advantage that I go away, for if I do not go away, the Advocate will not come to you; but if I go, I will send him to you."[3] The Advocate, or Helper, Jesus speaks of is his Spirit, the breath of God's own presence.

When you've been invited to a wedding, party, or dinner that you'll miss, you might express to the host in your RSVP, "I'll be there in spirit!" What do you really mean when you say that? What you're really saying is "I'm not going to be there." Jesus says to us, "I'll be there in Spirit!"—and he means it.

THROUGH THE CRACKS

Jesus' promise of God's Spirit is a window into how Christianity makes such deep sense of our whole selves. We've explored how, for the last few hundred years, those of us who inhabit the global West live within what philosopher Charles Taylor calls "the immanent frame"[4]—our working assumption about life is that this material world is all that exists. Nevertheless, we remain haunted by a stubborn thirst for transcendence that refuses to disappear. Like the roots of a great old oak tree that keep pressing up through the soil no matter how often a developer paves over them with concrete or asphalt, our yearning for transcendence keeps on pushing through the cracks of even the most secular life.

A bit ago, I was wandering through a neighborhood bookstore and happened on the burgeoning "spirituality" section. And there, neighboring the books on Zen meditation, mindfulness, and the spirituality of weight loss, was a then newly released book by Sam Harris. Harris, if you're not familiar with him, is a scientist and an author who has been a leading figure in the New Atheism movement. He's strident in his skepticism; in one of his typically provocative essays, Harris describes atheism as "nothing more than the noises reasonable people make when in the presence of religious dogma."[5] So I was startled to see that his most recent book at the time was titled *Waking Up: A Guide to Spirituality without Religion*. Here was Sam Harris, avowed nonbeliever, writing an entire book about the value of "self-transcendence" and the importance of all sorts of spiritual practices for one's life, from meditation to the use of psychedelic drugs.

Christianity would tell you that this stubborn desire for spiritual reality, which keeps pushing through the seams and cracks of an otherwise secular existence, resides in you because you were made for transcendence, for communion with the One who made you and all things. The Christian faith takes your whole self seriously. Being a follower of Jesus involves your intellect, and it involves responding to a set of historical facts—but it's also a matter of spiritual experience. It isn't irrational, but it also isn't only rational. The gospel of Jesus promises that you can share company with the God of the universe in such a way that he's closer to you than the breath in your own lungs.

COME-ALONGSIDE-ER, BREATH, FIRE

Jesus refers to God's Spirit as the "Helper" or the "Comforter." The Greek word used in these passages is *paraklētos*, which essentially means "the Come-Alongside-er" and is a legal term referring to one who comes alongside and makes the case for another. The church's great teachers have referred to the third person of the Trinity in a variety of ways. The early African church leader Tertullian referred to the Spirit as the "doctor veritatis"—the "truth doctor."[6] Augustine liked to talk about the Spirit as the "digitus Dei"—the "finger of God."[7] As we watch the moment when the Spirit is imparted to the company of Jesus, we see and hear some clues that give us a feel for what God's Spirit does in our lives.

In Acts 2, the first friends of Jesus are in the city of Jerusalem, still trying to make sense of their experiences of their risen Lord and Teacher and what it all means. It's Pentecost, an annual agricultural holiday and one of the main annual festivals of Jewish life. Then, the book of Acts says,

> suddenly from heaven there came a sound like the rush of a violent wind, and it filled the entire house where they were sitting. Divided tongues, as of fire, appeared among them, and a tongue rested on each of them. All of them were filled with the Holy Spirit and began to speak in other languages, as the Spirit gave them ability.[8]

First, there's the *wind*. The rushing wind recalls the Creation story, which begins the book of Genesis. God's *Spirit*—the word is *ruach* in Hebrew, which can mean "spirit," "breath," or "wind"—hovers, or flutters, over the soupy pre-Creation nothingness. Then there's the *fire*. The incandescent imagery of flame hearkens to the Exodus story: As God calls Moses to rescue a nation of helpless slaves, God's presence comes to Moses in the form of a bush that burns while never being consumed. The divine Glory leads the Israelite people from slavery through the long journey to freedom and to their promised home in the form of a pillar of fire. And it is fire that is later used in Jewish worship in the Temple to signify the brilliant glory of God's holy presence.

Putting all this together, we can begin to see what the Spirit does in the life of a Christian. The Spirit, to begin with, brings us God's very *presence*. Every baptized and believing follower of Jesus has in their depths the breath of God's own life; the life of every Christian is holy ground that houses the glory and brilliance of the Almighty! Even the most ordinary-looking Christian is a burning bush of God's own presence. The community of Jesus, thanks to the Spirit, shares in the company of God's own personal presence. This is the sense in which Jesus' cryptic words on his final night make sense as he assures his disciples that "my Father will love [you], and we will come to [you] and make our home with [you]."[9]

THE BODY OF JESUS CHRIST

In sharing the breath of Jesus' living presence, the community of Jesus also shares in his *vocation*. In Acts 2, after the nascent church community receives the Spirit, they're empowered to speak in other languages—not to babble gibberish but to announce in the native tongues of their neighbors "God's deeds of power" through the crucified and risen Lord.[10]

We who share the breath of Jesus are commissioned by God to live together, speak, and serve as the very presence of Jesus in the world. This is the sense in which various writers in the New Testament regularly refer to the church as "the body of Christ" and to individual Christians as "members" of this body. In today's culture, we use the language of membership in a commercial, transactional sense; we talk about being members of a gym or a frequent-flyer program or a wine-of-the-month club. But the language of Scripture is physical—it refers to Christians as members of "the body of Christ" in the way that your arm or leg is a "member" of your body. The church, in other words, with the breath of Jesus' presence residing in her, is called to live and serve as the ongoing physical, material presence of Christ in the world! Now, we have often fallen well short of that, but the church's track record doesn't negate her holy calling.

Finally, experiencing God's Spirit means coming to share in God's *future*. The Festival of Pentecost, at which God's Spirit takes up residence in Jesus' disciples, takes places fifty (the *pente* in *Pentecost* means "fifty") days after the Jewish Passover. It's a celebration of the first fruits of the year's harvest in which pilgrims would bring the first of their crops to Jerusalem to offer in thanks to God in hopeful anticipation of the full harvest to come. In the same way, the Spirit's presence in the church's life is a first fruit, a beginning taste, of our promised future. Elsewhere in the New Testament, the Spirit is referred to as a "down payment" of God's full, final rescue, which lies in our future.[11]

When I was a kid growing up in New Jersey, our family would often make the drive across the Walt Whitman Bridge to Veterans Stadium to watch a Phillies game or two together over the summer months. "The Vet" was Philadelphia's professional sports stadium from 1971 to 2003. Over those decades, generations of fans watched a few celebrated teams, and more than a few not-so-celebrated ones, play, lose, and win there. Children like me grew up, and grown-ups grew old, sitting in those soda-soaked seats year after year, cheering on the Phillies and the Eagles, Army or Navy, and Temple University. Once its demolition was scheduled in 2004, fans would scavenge, buy, and sell whatever pieces of the stadium they could: a brick, a seat, a sign, or a poster. For those who held on to them, those things were material pieces of their past, part of their story.

> **The Spirit is a taste of God's promised future that's ours in the present.**

The presence of God's Spirit in a Christian's life works in the same way but from the other direction. The Spirit is a piece of our Story that we hold on to—not from the past but from the future. The Spirit is a taste of God's promised future that's ours in the present. The healing, friendship, and communion with our Maker that Christians taste in our here and now is an appetizer course of what we will one day experience when God, in a fresh act of love and power, makes all things new and is "all in all."[12] The Spirit is the down payment on where God will ultimately bring the entire cosmos.

BE BORN AGAIN

Jesus once welcomes a curious religious leader named Nicodemus,[13] who turns up at his doorstep under cover of night. Nicodemus is intrigued by Jesus' healings and his strange, compelling teaching. And as they talk, Jesus tells Nicodemus that anyone who wants to experience a life with God goes through a transformation so dramatic that it's like a second birth. "You must be born [again]," Jesus tells him. Nicodemus, understandably, is confused: "Can one enter a second time into the mother's womb?" Jesus then elaborates. What he's describing is a transformation in one's depths, a spiritual renewal—being "born of the Spirit."[14] This is what being Jesus' follower means: experiencing a birth of God's own self into your life and, as such, a new beginning, a new identity so profound that it's like being birthed into a new life.

Some time ago, I saw a wall-sized ad that stopped me in my tracks. It hung on the large lobby wall of a downtown office building and featured an image of Michelangelo's famous plaster painting of God reaching out to humanity, which adorns the ceiling of the Sistine Chapel. There's God, reaching out, finger extended—and the imagery was positioned such that if you pressed the elevator button, you'd make contact with the proverbial digit of the Almighty.

And who was the Michelangelo advertisement for?

Dr. Kim's Plastic Surgery Associates, Floor 3, Office F.

The slogan, in bold block letters, across the bottom of the ad? *Be born again.*

What are they after, all the people who would press that button—and all the rest of us too? What are we looking for, with our obsessive self-improvement regimens, our fad diets, our meditation courses, our Botox, and our nose jobs?

Transformation. Transcendence. Spiritual connection. A new beginning.

We want to be born again.

The promise of the Christian gospel is that you can actually experience, in your day-to-day life, the breath of God's self in a way so profound that it's like undergoing birth again.

Jesus says to us, "I'll be there in Spirit"—and means it.

REFLECTION QUESTIONS

1. Is it difficult or easy for you to relate to God as Spirit? Why?

2. Which of the images for God's Spirit discussed in this chapter most resonate with you?

3. What is the most striking thing to you about what Christians say God's Spirit does in people's lives?

CHAPTER NINE

SHE'S A HARLOT, SHE'S MY MOTHER

Why Bother with the Church?

As to the Church, where else shall we go, except to the Bride of Christ, one flesh with Christ? Though she is a harlot at times, she is our Mother.

DOROTHY DAY

No one can have God as a father who does not have the Church as a mother.

CYPRIAN

"I can't do it anymore. I'm out."

Annie sat across from me at La Colombe's corner table. She shook her head, stirring her latte, wavy black hair cascading down over her angular glasses, voice cracking with heartbreak. Annie was a graduate law student who'd connected to our church two years prior. She was studying to become a public defender, and she'd led a number of our initiatives to serve Philly's food insecure and provide aid to the undocumented immigrant communities our church served. Annie was smart, passionate, large hearted. But she was growing increasingly uncomfortable with the idea of being a member of the church. "I love *our* church," she said wistfully. "I love the things we do; I love the people.

And I really do believe in Jesus. But I just can't take being part of *the* church anymore, and I don't know what that means for me. I just can't do it anymore."

This is what I hear from many who carry scars in their souls and bodies inflicted by those who claim to represent an institution that is "the body of Christ" in the world.[1] And I wonder this same thing too. I carry a few of those scars myself.

Recently I was having a conversation with a new attender at the church I now serve. As I asked about his spiritual journey, he replied, "I can sign on for most of the stuff we say in the Creed,[2] but the one I have a hard time with is the line about the church. I have no problem saying with a straight face, 'I believe in God, the Father almighty' and 'I believe in Jesus Christ, God's Son.' But 'I believe in . . . the church'? I don't know about the church."

I've spent more than two decades serving the church, and sometimes I don't know about the church either. As I've mentioned, after more than twenty years as a pastor, my own heart and soul bear the marks of the bigotry, hypocrisy, and ugliness of devout church folk.

In more than one unguarded moment, I've caught myself wondering the same.

Do I believe in the church?

Why bother?

Why not just do breathing exercises or go for a walk in the woods or take a scenic bike ride?

A NEW HUMANITY

We begin to unearth our need for the church as we reflect on our human hardwiring and on what we've discussed about the

One in whose image the Christian gospel insists we're made. Over the last century or so, psychologists, neurologists, and sociologists have begun increasingly to confirm what we've long known: We are hardwired for relationship.

In 1938, Harvard University launched what has become the longest-running longitudinal study on what makes people flourish. The study began with 724 participants—Harvard undergrads and boys from nearby disadvantaged Boston neighborhoods—and has grown to enfold the spouses of the original participants as well as thirteen hundred of their children and grandchildren. Researchers have tracked participants as they've grown up and grown old, fallen in and out of love, married and divorced, traversed professional successes and failures, found wealth and endured poverty, had children and died. And what have the researchers found? Robert Waldinger and Marc Schulz, current directors of the study, report that their vast research "brought us to a simple and profound conclusion: Good relationships lead to health and happiness."[3]

Relationships.

The reality of our innate relationality coheres in a deep way with the whole sweep of the Christian story.

Followers of Jesus believe that God, in his own being, is a community of loving relationship between Father, Son, and Holy Spirit. Love, we wager, is the beating heart of all reality.

And the agenda of our Creator, in coming among us in Christ, isn't just to rescue isolated individuals but to repair the fabric of our torn relationships with each other and to mend the whole creation. God means to reunite us with himself and with each other. To shape a new kind of human community.

This community—the church—is to be nothing less than a "new humanity,"[4] as the New Testament puts it.

So getting involved with God means getting involved with the other people God is also gracing and healing through Jesus. Lesslie Newbigin, a Christian leader in India and his native Great Britain during the twentieth century, wisely notices this connection. In one place in his writings, he addresses the question of why one needs to get involved with the inescapably muddled and imperfect people in the church if one wants to know God. Newbigin notes that, in the logic of the Christian gospel,

> there is . . . no private salvation, no salvation which does not involve us with one another. . . . God's saving revelation of himself does not come to us straight down from above—through the skylight, as we might say. In order to receive God's saving revelation we have to open the door to the neighbor whom he sends.[5]

If I want to open my life to experience God, I've got to open my door to other people.

A COMMUNITY OF GRACE

Human communities take shape in all sorts of ways, but no matter what the tribe, society, or cause, people tend to cluster together via some or another commonality: economic status or ideology or ethnicity, for example. And inherent in this tendency to bond together over what we have in common is to look down on those who are different from us—those who are "other." Miroslav Volf, a Croatian theologian who teaches at Yale, notes how human communities tend to use this, or often religion itself, as an "identity marker," which builds common ties of belonging among insiders and separates those with different identity markers.[6]

This was just as true in the first century as it is in the twenty-first. The Roman world Jesus and the early Christians knew was at least as sharply divided along lines of tribe, ethnicity, economic status, and religion as the one we inhabit today. The cultural, ethnic, and religious divide between Jewish and Gentile people, for example, was just as sharp as any we experience between classes, cultures, political ideologies, or nationalities today.

Listening to the Christian gospel in its first-century soil helps us realize what unique resources the Christian faith has to unite divided people groups. In a world where Jewish people loathe Gentiles (non-Jews) and think them inferior in every way, Paul proclaims that the dying and rising of Christ "has made both groups into one and has broken down the dividing wall, that is, the hostility between us."[7]

How can that be?

It's because of the core of Christianity itself. Unlike other ideologies—and even unlike how religion itself, broadly speaking, works—what draws together the Christian community is not that everyone shares a similar culture, ethnicity, economic status, or background. It's not that members of the Christian community have any of our usual identity markers in common. And it's not that these members automatically share a common moral vocabulary about what people ought to do or not do with our lives.

What creates the Christian community is that it's founded

not on what we do or don't do but on what God has done in Christ.

What we have in common isn't ideology or background or nationality—it's grace.

Our common identity marker is the Cross.

There's a poignant piece of short fiction in the *New Yorker* that depicts the beauty and difficulty of this dynamic. "The Long Black Line," authored by John L'Heureux, follows Finn, a young man who's a newcomer—a novice—to a Roman Catholic Jesuit order (a community of Christians who commit to live together in community and give themselves to prayer and service). On his first day, he meets Brother Reilly, who gives him a tour of the facilities. The men quickly get under each other's skin. Things escalate quickly. When at one point Brother Reilly turns and addresses him as "Brother Finn," Finn attempts a bit of friendliness: "Just call me Finn. Brother Finn creeps me out." L'Heureux writes:

> Brother Reilly, with a show of patience, explained that in the Jesuit order all novices were called Brother. He pointed them out—Brother Quirk, Brother Matthews, Brother Lavelle, etc. And then, lapsing from charity, he added, "You are now my brother, Brother Finn, and I don't like it any more than you do."[8]

The crucified love of Jesus gathers a family out of people who'd otherwise be strangers or enemies. Grace brings me into a

What creates the Christian community is that it's founded not on what we do or don't do but on what God has done in Christ.

community of people who are now my brothers and sisters—like it or not.

HARLOT MOTHER

So what to do with Annie's aching disillusionment over the church? What do we do with the reality that this embracing vision of God's grace gathering a unique kind of human community seems so far from what we see of the church on the news or encounter when we darken the doors of one ourselves?

Maybe the chasm between vision and reality shouldn't be so surprising to us.

The church is a collection of beautifully diverse people, loved and claimed by grace, yes. But the church is also a collection of, well . . . sinners. Every person in a Christian congregation is a sinner. And they don't stop being one when they're baptized and join a local congregation. In fact, as we've discussed, acknowledging that you're a "miserable offender" is pretty much the entry requirement for Christianity. The only kind of churches that exist are ones comprised entirely of sinners. So maybe it shouldn't shock us that when groups of sinners gather, they continue to sin against God and each other.

The late Eugene Peterson, a pastor and author, puts this frankly in a book for Christian leaders:

> The biblical fact is that there are no [perfect] churches. There are, instead, communities of sinners, gathered before God week after week in towns and villages all over the world. The Holy Spirit gathers them and does his work in them. In these communities of sinners, one

of the sinners is called pastor and given a designated responsibility in the community.⁹

As a church leader, I feel the pain of that gap between what we're supposed to be (a new humanity!) and what we are (a highly dysfunctional aggregation of sinners). As I've mentioned, I've been bruised by the hypocrisy, wrong, and failings of the church. But I've dealt others some bruises too. I didn't stop being a sinner when I started being a pastor. And so, inescapably, there are lots of people I've let down or hurt in some way or disappointed in my years as a minister.

In Christian language, both individual Christians and church communities are simul justus et peccator—simultaneously saint and sinner. Loved and graced, yes. But also still flawed, imperfect, and constantly in need of mercy. Following Jesus on the road into new life, to be sure. But not there yet either.

The Christian Scriptures paint a surprisingly realistic picture of this tension. Many of the books of the New Testament were originally a letter written from a pastor to a new local Christian community in some or another city, trying to sort out what it looked like for them to live their new life in Jesus together. When we read them now, it's like listening to one side of a conversation. And the picture of these communities that comes into view is not of utopias. It'll likely look (perhaps depressingly) familiar.

In some of them, some groups refused to welcome others or sit down to meals with them. In others, richer members would feast and get drunk while poorer ones went hungry. They argued angrily over matters of belief and ethics. Early Christian communities struggled with the same varieties of favoritism, backbiting, clique making, gossip, and slander that Christian communities do today. And they mired themselves in moral and sexual dysfunction, just as so many Christians do today. The apostle Paul even had to tell a person in one particular church that he needed to stop sleeping with his mother-in-law since he was a church member.[10]

We're saints now because of grace but, until God finishes his work, still very much sinners.

Simul justus et peccator.

Dorothy Day was an impassioned follower of Jesus who became a founding leader of the Catholic Worker Movement. Her faith-fueled activism sought to improve the conditions of factory workers, provide aid for the poor, and advocate for pacifism. Her life of service was rooted deeply in her faith, so she often struggled with the dialectic between what the church is called to be and do and the reality she saw all too often. On one occasion, expressing her frustration over other church leaders' response to violence in Vietnam, she wrote, "As to the Church, where else shall we go, except to the Bride of Christ, one flesh with Christ? *Though she is a harlot at times, she is our Mother.*"[11]

That's the inescapable paradox of the church.

She's a harlot.

She's our mother.

SEMPER REFORMANDA

None of this is to excuse or minimize the catastrophic harm the church has done in millennia past, or in our present. I'm in no way shrugging off the pain you may have experienced in an institution that bears the Name, but perhaps not the heart, of Christ Jesus.

I'm saying the opposite, actually. We need to hear the cries of those who have been stepped on, taken advantage of, and left outside the walls of the church as a call to go deeper in to the heart of the One we're called to reflect.

The particular tradition of the Christian church I inhabit is the Reformed Church; it traces its beginnings as a renewal movement in sixteenth-century Europe committed to addressing the corruption and abuses of the church in her own day and helping followers of Jesus recover the Good News of grace that lies at the heart of our faith. One of the slogans that grew out of this movement in its beginnings is still very apropos to the church's situation today, five centuries later: *Ecclesia reformata, semper reformanda.* It means "The church reformed, always reforming."

As communities filled with people who are at once beloved and broken, we're always on the journey of repentance and renewal.

Always reforming.

Always seeking to become more like the One who embraces us with the scars of grace, who's "gentle and humble in heart," who gives rest to the weary and freedom to the burdened.[12]

NO BODY BUT YOURS

There's another dimension to this too. Jesus didn't write a book—he commissioned a community of people to live and announce his Way in the world.[13]

Before his ascension to take his seat on the throne of the

universe, Jesus promised that he would continue working, healing, and teaching in the world until the day in which he would make all things new. And the way that Jesus committed himself to work in the world was through the lives of his followers. In John 20, there's this fascinating moment in which, on the evening of the first Easter, Jesus sneaks up on a despondent room full of his friends, breathes his own Spirit into each of them, and then gives them these marching orders: "As the Father has sent me, so I send you."[14]

In other words, it is through communities of imperfect, unimpressive followers of Jesus—the church—that the living Jesus is on the move in our world today.

Jesus' way of embracing the person in your department at work who's sure that they're too far gone for grace? You and me.

Jesus' plan to care for the kids in the housing project a few miles down the road from you, enduring daily traumas of violence and neglect? You and me.

Jesus' strategy to bring clean water to the village in South Sudan that has none and that has been torn apart by tribal warfare? You and me.

The church.

Teresa of Ávila was a sixteenth-century mystic and follower of Jesus deeply involved in reform work in the church of her day. This poem, attributed to her, puts the vocation that all of us who comprise Jesus' church share in vivid fashion:

Christ has no body but yours,
No hands, no feet on earth but yours,
Yours are the eyes with which he looks
Compassion on this world,

> *Yours are the feet with which he walks to do good,*
> *Yours are the hands, with which he blesses all the world.*
> *Yours are the hands, yours are the feet,*
> *Yours are the eyes, you are his body.*
> *Christ has no body now but yours,*
> *No hands, no feet on earth but yours,*
> *Yours are the eyes with which he looks*
> *compassion on this world.*
> *Christ has no body now on earth but yours.*[15]

This is why, despite everything, I believe in the church.

THE UNCLE BILL QUANDARY

So what do you do when you're disillusioned with the harlot mother who is the church?

Even for me as a Christian minister, there are moments when it's hard not to just walk away from the whole mess.

But here's the quandary.

I need other people to live a whole, full human life. I can't become fully myself by myself. I can biologically exist, sure—but I won't find the flourishing version of life intended by our Maker on my own. I need people for that. A larger community in which to belong. Dare I say it?—even the human community Jesus draws together: the church.

I bet you do too. It's tempting to sever every relationship with someone who's flawed, jettison every community that's imperfect, and reject every institution around me that's dysfunctional.

My wife, Monica, has an aunt who, when she was a young woman, married this guy named Bill. He was a towering, immense man who wore his long, wispy black hair in a ponytail. When our family used to take family photos at Thanksgiving or Christmas, he'd always be there in the back-center of the group, hulking over everyone else.

After a while, things didn't work out between this aunt and Bill, and they ended their marriage. In addition to the normal difficulties of divorce, there was another dilemma: What to do with these years of family photos that all featured Bill, presiding in the back-center? This, after all, was long before the days of Photoshop, which now lets us digitally erase an inconvenient presence from a picture with a few swipes of the mouse and the click of a button.

Monica's grandma, ever a resourceful woman, came up with a practical solution. In the coming years, we'd see her pictures of our family at those former holiday gatherings with a big, round hole right in the middle where Bill used to be. Grandma just took some kitchen shears to those photos and scissored him right out.

Ever since, our family has literally had a Bill-shaped hole in it.

I think often about those old Bill-less pictures. It's tempting, when I disagree vehemently with someone in my church, or when one of her leaders acts in a way contrary to the Spirit of Jesus, to just cut them right out of my life. To take the proverbial scissors to the bond between us and be done with it.

The problem is, after a while, my life starts to have an awful lot of holes in it. And not enough other people.

In his lectures, Lesslie Newbigin observed that, alone among the founding figures of the world's major faiths, Jesus of Nazareth didn't leave behind a book.

He left behind a community.[16]

This means that, from the very first Easter morning, the way God saw fit to bring the Good News of the risen Christ to a blighted world was *through people*.

People are God's strange way of working in the world.

God came near us and disclosed himself to us by becoming a person.

Jesus commissioned the news of grace to be carried to the corners of the earth by means of a community of people (and not an especially impressive one at that).

I need the voices of other people to announce to me the Jesus Story of God's deliverance.

It takes another flesh-and-blood person to splash the baptismal water into my life and those of my children; to promise us, "For you Jesus Christ came into the world; for you he died and for you he conquered death."[17] To pronounce that all of us marked by the waters of baptism are claimed by God's promise and made his own.

Some embodied soul needs to consecrate bread and wine and offer them to me for me to partake the holy mysteries of Christ's body and blood at Holy Communion.

There's no app for that stuff.

And it takes actual people to do all the rest of what makes up life in company with God's family too: assuring me of grace when I'm sure I've screwed up one too many times. Offering me wisdom when I'm in danger of doing something foolish. Showing up with wine or whiskey or a casserole on the best days, when there's something to celebrate. And on the worst days, when there's a tragedy to mourn. And all the innumerable other ways I need God's people to help me learn the ropes of life with God.

In other words, though she's at times deeply unfaithful, I need the church.

I bet you do too.

REFLECTION QUESTIONS

1. Is it difficult for you to trust the church? If so, why?

2. This chapter provides reasons for embracing the church despite her flaws. How do you respond to this way of thinking?

3. What is unique about the kind of community that the Christian Good News creates?

CHAPTER TEN
DURABLE WELFARE
Hope for Tomorrow, Hope for Today

*I look forward to the resurrection of the dead
and the life of the world to come.*
THE NICENE CREED

*I wake up sometimes way in the night and
I know as certain as death that there aint nothin short
of the second comin of Christ that can slow this train.*
Sheriff Ed Tom Bell in **CORMAC McCARTHY,**
No Country for Old Men

In their November 2007 issue, to commemorate their one hundred and fiftieth birthday, the *Atlantic* commissioned an eclectic set of thinkers, artists, and journalists to pen brief pieces on "the future of the American idea." In a punchy essay entitled "God-Drunk Society," atheist author Sam Harris put his finger on one of the troubles many twenty-first-century people have with Christianity:

[Many Americans] apparently believe that Jesus will return someday and orchestrate the end of the world with his magic powers. This hankering for a denominational, spiritual oblivion is not a good bet, much less a useful idea.

And yet, abject superstition of this kind engorges our nation from sea to shining sea. . . .

It need not be so. . . . We could also lead the world in wise environmental policies, scientific education, medical research, aid to developing countries, and every other project relevant to the durable welfare of humanity.[1]

For Harris, and for many people, the trouble with the Christian teaching about "last things" isn't just that it seems to him out-of-date and superstitious; it's also that he thinks the Christian view of our ultimate destiny counterproductive—where people could invest their intellect and energy into the pressing problems of the world, Christians content themselves with theorizing about the times, dates, and weather conditions of the second coming of Jesus.

It embarrasses me a bit to acknowledge that, within certain strains of American Christianity over the last century, there has indeed been a bizarre hankering over the "end times."[2] One of the sad ironies of this is that, in Jesus' own teachings, he insists on the impossibility of knowing the hows, whens, and wheres of God's final acts.[3] And so, in the last portion of this guided tour of Christianity's essential teachings, I hope to untangle a couple of knots and clear up a few misconceptions. And I hope to help you see that there's no community of people with more motivation to be dedicated to "the durable welfare of humanity" than those who live in view of "the resurrection of the dead and the life of the world to come."[4]

RESURRECTION-SHAPED HOPE

The Christian vision of our destiny takes its contour and shape from the resurrection of Jesus on Easter morning. The Resurrection is both the means and the model of the Christian faith and life.[5] N. T. Wright puts it succinctly: Christians believe that "God [is] going to do for the whole cosmos what he had done for Jesus at Easter."[6] The ultimate hope, then, of people shaped by the gospel is that of *resurrection*. This is what untold millions of people, in cathedrals and storefronts, chapels and country churches affirm week by week: "I look forward to the resurrection of the dead and the life of the world to come."

Think again of the large story arc of the Bible that we've been reflecting on. The Creator shapes a good cosmos, in which God and humanity, heaven and earth, are connected and flourishing. Sin and death, in turn, fracture the interlocking nexus of relationships between God and humanity, between people, and between people and their work and the material world. The expansive, winding Story of redemption that comprises the biblical narrative and comes to a climax in Jesus, then, is all about God restoring, reuniting, and renewing his own good creation.

The Scriptures use a number of images to portray the Christian hope. In the last chapters of Revelation, John pictures this Great Day as a reunion of heaven and earth, a renewed city, and a cosmic marriage:

> Then I saw a new heaven and a new earth; for the first heaven and the first earth had passed away, and the sea was no more. And I saw the holy city, the new Jerusalem, coming down out of heaven from God,

prepared as a bride adorned for her husband. And I heard a loud voice from the throne saying,

> "See, the home of God is among mortals.
> He will dwell with them as their God;
> they will be his peoples,
> and God himself will be with them;
> he will wipe every tear from their eyes.
> Death will be no more;
> mourning and crying and pain will be no more,
> for the first things have passed away."[7]

Notice here what this vivid vision pictures: not people going off to "heaven"; but heaven, as it were, coming to earth. Much of John's imagery is drawn together from the ancient poetry of the prophet Isaiah. And Isaiah similarly depicts a day in which God will once and for all undo death and renew his good creation forever:

> In days to come
>   the mountain of the Lord's house
> shall be established as the highest of the mountains . . .
> all the nations shall stream to it.
>   Many peoples shall come and say,
> "Come, let us go up to the mountain of the Lord,
>   to the house of the God of Jacob;
> that he may teach us his ways
>   and that we may walk in his paths."
> . . . He shall judge between the nations,
>   and shall arbitrate for many peoples;

> they shall beat their swords into plowshares,
> > and their spears into pruning hooks;
> nation shall not lift up sword against nation,
> > neither shall they learn war any more.[8]
>
> For I am about to create new heavens
> > and a new earth;
> the former things shall not be remembered
> > or come to mind.
> But be glad and rejoice forever
> > in what I am creating;
> for I am about to create Jerusalem as a joy,
> > and its people as a delight. . . .
> The wolf and the lamb shall feed together,
> > the lion shall eat straw like the ox;
> > but the serpent—its food shall be dust!
> They shall not hurt or destroy
> > on all my holy mountain,
>
> > > > says the LORD.[9]

Isaiah depicts a future in which the God of life will undo death and violence once and for all, overcome evil (notice the mention of the serpent), and dwell with his rescued people forever.

In his discussion of Jesus' resurrection in 1 Corinthians 15, which we spent time in earlier, Paul employs the agricultural image of a great harvest to picture this promised moment. He calls the raising of Jesus the "first fruits" of a great future harvest, in which God will raise all his people from death, having broken its power in Christ, and into a future in which "God [will] be all in all."¹⁰

Putting these various images together, we see that Christian hope is resurrection shaped: In other words, we don't look for a day in which we'll be evacuated from this evil, dirty, material life; rather, we trust ourselves to a future in which God will raise us beyond death into a healed, renewed, God-drenched future. Our final hope is about resurrection, not evacuation; new creation, not oblivion.

Our final hope is about resurrection, not evacuation; new creation, not oblivion.

JUDGMENT AND RESCUE

Christians believe that, on that promised Day, the risen Jesus "will come again to judge the living and the dead."¹¹ The themes of resurrection and new life—and judgment—find their way into all the various scriptural and creedal depictions of our ultimate future. God, the Scriptures promise again and again, will one day make a final end of death, violence, evil, and sin. God will save his people *from judgment* through the rescuing work of Christ, but he won't save his people or his creation *without judgment*.

The idea of God judging is of course deeply off-putting to many in the twenty-first century. I remember having a conversation with a new visitor to the church I serve in which he told me in no uncertain terms that he was an outsider to the faith, only beginning to investigate the story of Jesus. He then added, "I guess the main thing that I find off-putting about Christianity is all the smiting. I just can't get behind all the smiting."

It's interesting, then, to note that in the Scriptures, God's judgment is depicted as something to be longed for and celebrated. Listen to Psalm 98, for example:

Let the sea roar, and all that fills it;
    the world and those who live in it.
Let the floods clap their hands;
    let the hills sing together for joy
at the presence of the LORD, for he is coming
    to judge the earth.
He will judge the world with righteousness,
    and the peoples with equity.[12]

The ancient poetry of the Psalms portrays creation itself cheering on the judgment of God, clapping its hands and shouting at the top of its lungs. Why is this? Because God's judgment is an expression of his faithful, dogged love. God judges because God cares, not because he doesn't.

Miroslav Volf is a theologian at Yale who grew up amid the horrors of ethnic cleansing in the Yugoslav Wars. In a landmark book he authored called *Exclusion and Embrace*, in which he reflects on the Christian gospel in light of his own life experiences, he calls into question our modern, Western assumption that a God of love couldn't judge and that belief in a God who judges evil leads to oppression and violence:

> One could object that it is not worthy of God to wield the sword. Is God not love, long-suffering and all-powerful love? A counter-question could go something like this: Is it not a bit too arrogant to presume

that our contemporary sensibilities about what is compatible with God's love are so much healthier than those of the people of God throughout the whole history of Judaism and Christianity? . . . If God were *not angry* at injustice and deception and *did not* make the final end to violence God would not be worthy of our worship.[13]

It is, in other words, *because* God is a God of love that he refuses to ignore violence, shrug off genocide, look the other way at exploitation. It is because the Creator is committed to healing the good creation that he promises to make a final end of violence, to put things right once and for all, to overthrow human greed and arrogance, to put death itself to death. A God who doesn't judge doesn't care.

Cormac McCarthy's harrowing novel *No Country for Old Men* is set along the Texas-Mexico border and unfolds across the backdrop of the narcotics trade. In one moment, county sheriff Ed Tom Bell is musing on all the heartbreak, evil, and death that the drug trade has visited on his little town. As he does, he says, "I wake up sometimes way in the night and I know as certain as death that there aint nothin short of the second comin of Christ that can slow this train. I dont know what is the use of me layin awake over it. But I do."[14]

Christians believe that no matter how dark the news headlines get, no matter how bleak the state of affairs when you look at your news browser (or in the mirror), there will be a final end to all death, ugliness, and hate: the second coming of Christ, to judge the living and the dead.

TOMORROW TODAY

The vocation of God's people, then, with this glorious future in view, is this: to live our todays in light of that dazzling Tomorrow. Christians are called to live our present in a way that anticipates the world's promised future.

It's striking to listen to the implications that the biblical writers draw out of the various pictures given of God's future, final work. In Isaiah 2, for example, after the prophet pictures the nations gathering around God and swords being beat into plowshares, what does he say? "Come, let us walk in the light of the LORD!"[15] In other words: "Let this vision of tomorrow shape your life today!"

In 1 Corinthians 15, as Paul concludes his masterful explication of the Resurrection and what it means, how does he finish? "Well, folks, since Jesus is raised from the dead, lock yourselves away and ignore the problems of the world until God melts it all down"? No! This is his call to the church:

> Therefore, my beloved, be steadfast, immovable, always excelling in the work of the Lord, because you know that in the Lord your labor is not in vain.[16]

You know that in the Lord your labor is not in vain.

You're not arranging deck chairs on the Titanic. You're not repairing a car that's ultimately headed to the junkyard. You're not restoring a piece of art that's about to be thrown out.

And so Christians live their present lives anticipating and, in the divine alchemy of God, *participating now* in that ultimate future.

Think again with me about Sam Harris's objection that

Christians, because of our future hope, don't care about the durable welfare of the world. Think again about my friend Aaron and the dilemma he shared with me in our neighborhood pub's back corner.

Why give your money away, why spend your time healing sick bodies, why campaign for educational opportunities for the disadvantaged, if life is ultimately meaningless and nothing more than a cosmic blip ending in extinction?

Conversely: Who could possibly care more about the durable welfare of the world than Christians? Christians believe that this world is good and God's idea. Christians believe that God so loved this world that he took up the stuff of material life in the person of Jesus of Nazareth. And Christians believe that one day God will finish what he began at the empty tomb of Jesus, undoing death and decay once and for all and raising all his people and all his cosmos into healed new life forever.

And so Christians love enemies. And build hospitals. And cathedrals. Christians paint and dance. Christians give their money away to drill clean water wells and to build affordable homes for those without housing. Christians write music and campaign to end human trafficking. Christians feed hungry bodies, educate minds, and offer hope to bruised and battered hearts.

Because we know that, in the risen Lord, none of it is in vain. It all matters. It all lasts. In the resurrecting power of God, it all lasts forever.

TREE OF LIFE

Last year, while traveling through London, I had a free afternoon that I spent wandering the exhibit halls of the British

Museum. As I rounded a corner into Room 25, there was an immense sculpture that immediately arrested my attention. The piece depicted an enormous, towering tree made of metal scraps. As I read the history of its creation, I learned that it had been created in Mozambique. Following their long, bloody civil war, there was a Christian bishop named Dinis Sengulane who led a campaign that saw some six hundred thousand turn in their guns, which were in turn decommissioned. Four artists then used the materials of these decommissioned weapons to forge this towering sculpture of a tree.

Its title? *Tree of Life*, named after the tree that features in the final chapter of Revelation as a symbol of God's healing power and forever life.

It's a picture of the hope loosed into a violent, dark world on Easter Sunday: that what God did in raising Jesus he will one day do for the cosmos. That the God who could take the wood of an instrument of death and transform it into a tree of life that will one day bring everlasting life to the world. That God will one day refashion pain into peace, repurpose violence into healing, transfigure death into resurrection life.

REFLECTION QUESTIONS

1. What are your perceptions around what Christians believe about the "end times"?

2. How are our beliefs about the future connected to how we live today?

3. What are some of the implications of the Christian belief in resurrection that you resonate with?

EPILOGUE
Not Lying Anymore

Every Sunday, many of the world's over two billion Christians rise to their feet, declare, "I believe . . . ," and recite the Apostles' Creed. In favelas in Brazil, cathedrals across Europe, ramshackle storefronts in Los Angeles, and countless other settings circling the globe, followers of Jesus say a translation of the Christian credo—that densely packed shorthand of the narrative of God and the cosmos that we stake our lives upon. The Christian creeds have been shared between candidates for baptism in caves, with Roman noblewomen, with African chieftains, with union drywallers on Long Island, from parents to children and to their children, around the world and across millennia. My church joins the wider Christian family in this formative practice, and I'll never forget the way it marked Abigail's pilgrimage into faith.

The first time I talked with Abigail, she was waiting for me in a neighborhood café near her apartment, sitting at a table set against the back corner of the coffee shop where we had agreed to meet. She had emailed me the week prior, introduced herself, let me know she had just begun attending our church's worship services, and asked if we could meet sometime to talk. She waved at me through the crowd of college students clumped together at tables, suit-clad professionals stopping in for caffeine en route to the office, and young moms herding strollers and toddlers. As I sat down, took a sip of my Americano, and said hello, Abigail wasted no time telling me that she was an atheist. A Harvard-educated medical researcher, she had just taken a position at a recently opened firm. We hadn't been together more than a few minutes when she told me, "Listen, I need to be honest: I do not understand how any educated, rational person in the twenty-first century believes in God or Jesus or any of that lot. I think it's equivalent to believing in aliens or the Loch Ness Monster."

I thanked her for her honesty, paused for a moment, and then asked her: "Then why do you bother coming to worship?"

"I'm not sure. That's what I'm trying to figure out."

I offered to Abigail that I'd be happy to connect whenever she'd like to continue our conversation, and we went our separate ways. Most Sundays, I'd see her: plastered to the pew on the back wall, she'd listen to the call to worship and confession, the hymns and Scriptures and sermon. She'd stand silently as we rose to our feet and recited the Creed. And then she'd slip out the sanctuary door as other worshipers began making their way forward to receive Communion.

Every month or two, Abigail would drop me an email and ask to have another cup of coffee. I'd listen to her questions and talk with her about what she'd heard in a hymn line or the sermon that had either intrigued or puzzled or offended. Often I'd leave wondering if I'd said anything that even made sense to her.

EPILOGUE

After a number of these meetings, Abigail sent me an email: "Can we plan another coffee soon?" A few mornings later, we sat at our usual table in our habitual places. And after a bit of small talk, Abigail started in: "Jared, I have a problem, and I need your help to figure out what to do about it."

"What's that, Abigail?"

"Well, here it is: You know how we stand in worship after the sermon every week and say the Creed together?"

"Yeah?"

"Well, it occurred to me recently that when I started coming to church, I would stand up and listen to everyone, and I thought it was all foolishness, a bunch of fables and lies. But, recently, when that moment comes in the service, I've started saying the Creed with everyone. And I'm at the point now where, when we say it, I don't think I'm lying anymore. What should I do?"

I swallowed hard. "Well, Abigail, I know I'm running the risk of alarming you, but here's what I think: I think you're becoming a Christian. I think you ought to get baptized and we should welcome you into the church."

Abigail leaned back in her chair, exhaled a heavy sigh, and looked at some spot on the ceiling above and behind my head for a few interminable minutes. Then she looked at me, sighed again, and said:

"Shoot. I thought you'd probably say that . . . All right. Let's do it."

That Easter, Abigail knelt in our sanctuary; we splashed baptismal water on her in the name of Father, Son, and Spirit; and we cheered her into the community of sinners and saints, believers and doubters that we all are.

I hope that, in some way, this book will aid as a conversation partner to you, wherever you are in your own journey, whatever your own process looks like. My shameless desire is that, whatever the road looks like for you, you'll be able to say with Abigail, "I believe—and I'm not lying about it" . . . to yourself or to anybody else.

ACKNOWLEDGMENTS

To all the sinners and saints, believers and skeptics, that I've had the privilege of serving as a pastor: Thank you for the holy privilege of accompanying you on your journey, and for accompanying me along mine.

To the Eugene Peterson Center for Christian Imagination, Western Theological Seminary, and especially Chuck DeGroat, Winn Collier, Marilyn McEntyre, and John Blase: Thanks to each of you for helping me find my voice.

Thanks to First Presbyterian Church in North Palm Beach, Florida, for the time, support, and encouragement that made this book possible.

To David Zimmerman, Deborah Sáenz, and the team at NavPress: I'm grateful for your guidance and support, and that you took a risk on a rookie writer.

To sacred friends too numerous to name, and to my dad, my brothers, and Brennan, Kuyper, and Rae: The best of who I am and anything I say derive from you.

NOTES

INTRODUCTION | FOR THOSE WHO FRET ABOUT IT
1. *True Detective*, season 1, episode 3, "The Locked Room," written by Nic Pizzolatto, directed by Cary Joji Fukunaga, aired January 26, 2014, on HBO.
2. Dietrich Bonhoeffer, *Psalms: The Prayer Book of the Bible* (Minneapolis: Fortress Press, 1974), 13.
3. Psalm 13:1-2, Robert Alter, *The Hebrew Bible: A Translation with Commentary* (New York: W. W. Norton, 2019), 3:47–48.
4. Psalm 73:3-5, Alter, *Hebrew Bible*, 3:176.
5. Psalm 22:2-3, Alter, *Hebrew Bible*, 3:66.
6. Mark 15:34.
7. Luke 24:5.
8. Luke 24:11.
9. I have changed the names, and at times life details, of most of the people mentioned in this book, though they and their stories are real.
10. David Mizner, "Reporting an Explosive Truth: The *Boston Globe* and Sexual Abuse in the Catholic Church," CSJ-09-0011, Knight Case Studies Initiative, Columbia University, accessed January 21, 2025, https://casestudies.ccnmtl.columbia.edu/case/ReportinganExplosiveTruth.
11. Amanda Casanova, "Grace Community Church Leaders under Fire for 'Excommunicating' Wife Who Refused to Stay with Abusive Husband," Crosswalk, updated March 24, 2022, https://www.crosswalk.com/headlines/contributors/guest-commentary/grace-community-church-leaders-under-fire-for-excommunicating-wife-who-refused-to-stay-with-abusive-husband.html.

CHAPTER ONE | HEIMA

1. XL Recordings, "Sigur Ros—*Heima* Trailer," September 26, 2007, YouTube, https://www.youtube.com/watch?v=EuftN2ViiN4.
2. See Genesis 1:27.
3. Frederick Buechner, *The Longing for Home: Recollections and Reflections* (New York: HarperCollins, 2009), 110.
4. Sigal Samuel, "Atheists Are Sometimes More Religious than Christians," *Atlantic*, May 31, 2018, https://www.theatlantic.com/international/archive/2018/05/american-atheists-religious-european-christians/560936.
5. John Bunyan, as quoted by Ann Charters, introduction to *On the Road*, by Jack Kerouac (New York: Penguin Books, 2003), xiv–xv.
6. Charters, introduction to *On the Road*, xxi.
7. David Bellos, introduction to *The Plague, The Fall, Exile and the Kingdom, and Selected Essays*, by Albert Camus (New York: Everyman's Library, 2004), xiv.
8. Bellos, introduction to *The Plague, The Fall*, xvi.
9. Camus, *The Plague, The Fall*, 225.
10. Fyodor Dostoevsky, *The Brothers Karamazov*, trans. Richard Pevear and Larissa Volokhonsky (New York: Everyman's Library, 1992), 589.
11. Dante Alighieri, *The Divine Comedy: Inferno, Purgatorio, Paradiso*, trans. Allen Mandelbaum (New York: Everyman's Library, 1995), 59.
12. C. S. Lewis, *The Weight of Glory* (New York: HarperOne, 2001), 29–30.
13. Lewis, *Weight of Glory*, 30–31.
14. J. R. R. Tolkien, "On Fairy-Stories," in *Tree and Leaf, Including Mythopoeia and The Homecoming of Beorhtnoth Beorhthelm's Son* (London: Harper Collins, 2001), 33.
15. Genesis 2:25.
16. Cornelius Plantinga Jr., *Engaging God's World: A Christian Vision of Faith, Learning, and Living* (Grand Rapids: Eerdmans, 2002), 14–15.
17. Genesis 2:17.
18. Genesis 3:23-24.
19. For example, Hosea 9:15-17.
20. Genesis 3:9.

CHAPTER TWO | CURRENTS

1. "U.S. Public Becoming Less Religious," Pew Research Center, November 3, 2015, https://www.pewresearch.org/religion/2015/11/03/u-s-public-becoming-less-religious. This documents findings of Pew's 2014 Religious Landscape Study.
2. "About Three-in-Ten U.S. Adults Are Now Religiously Unaffiliated," Pew

NOTES

Research Center, December 14, 2021, https://www.pewresearch.org/religion/2021/12/14/about-three-in-ten-u-s-adults-are-now-religiously-unaffiliated.
3. Jason DeRose, "Religious 'Nones' Are Now the Largest Single Group in the U.S.," *All Things Considered*, NPR, January 24, 2024, https://www.npr.org/2024/01/24/1226371734/religious-nones-are-now-the-largest-single-group-in-the-u-s.
4. Charles Taylor, *A Secular Age* (Cambridge, MA: Belknap Press of Harvard University Press, 2007), 22.
5. Lesslie Newbigin, "Can the West Be Converted?," *Princeton Seminary Bulletin* 6, no. 1 (1985): 25–37, https://commons.ptsem.edu/id/princetonsemina6119prin_0-dmd008. Newbigin credits Peter L. Berger with introducing the concept of plausibility structures in *The Heretical Imperative: Contemporary Possibilities of Religious Affirmation*.
6. This analogy is borrowed from Alister McGrath, *The Unknown God: Searching for Spiritual Fulfilment* (Grand Rapids: Eerdmans, 1999), 20–21.
7. Sigmund Freud, quoted in McGrath, *Unknown God*, 22.
8. McGrath, *Unknown God*, 20.
9. Defenses of the Christian gospel have been penned as early as the second century AD. The classic comprehensive Christian exploration of the philosophical and rational reasons for belief in God can be found in Thomas Aquinas, *Summa Contra Gentiles* (thirteenth century AD). The quintessential modern articulation of the rational reasons for belief in the Christian faith can be found in C. S. Lewis, *Mere Christianity* (1952). And some of the foremost contemporary philosophical and scientific defenses of Christian belief in God can be found in Michael J. Murray, ed., *Reason for the Hope Within* (1998); Alvin Plantinga, *Warranted Christian Belief* (2000); and Francis S. Collins, *The Language of God: A Scientist Presents Evidence for Belief* (2007).
10. Blaise Pascal, *Pascal's Pensées*, trans. Martin Turnell (New York: Harper & Brothers, 1962), 234.
11. I borrow this phrase from Alvin Plantinga, in *Warranted Christian Belief*.
12. Francis Collins, quoted in Steve Paulson, "The Believer," Salon, August 7, 2006, https://www.salon.com/2006/08/07/collins_6.
13. C. S. Lewis, *Mere Christianity* (New York: Harper Collins, 2001), 38–39.
14. David Bazan, "In Stitches," track 10 on *Curse Your Branches*, Barsuk Records, 2009.

CHAPTER THREE | YHWH

1. "The Archbishop Writes to Lulu, Aged 6, about God," archived website of Dr Rowan Williams, accessed March 24, 2025, http://rowanwilliams.archbishopofcanterbury.org/articles.php/2389/the-archbishop-writes-to-lulu-aged-6-about-god.html. Originally published as Alex Renton, "A Letter to God—and a Reply from Lambeth," *Times*, March 11, 2011.
2. Raymond E. Brown, *The Gospel according to John, I–XII*, The Anchor Bible, vol. 29, bk. 1 (Garden City, NY: Doubleday, 1982), 4–37.
3. Brown, *Gospel according to John*, 4. This is Brown's translation of John 1:18.
4. See John 1:18 in the ESV, NIV, and NRSV, for instance.
5. Colossians 1:15, 19-20.
6. Genesis 1:1.
7. From the Belgic Confession, article 2.
8. E. A. Speiser, *Genesis*, The Yale Anchor Bible, vol. 1 (Garden City, NY: Doubleday, 1964), 10–12.
9. Cornelius Plantinga Jr., *Engaging God's World: A Christian Vision of Faith, Learning, and Living* (Grand Rapids: Eerdmans, 2002), 23.
10. Note the sixfold repetition of "And God said . . . and it was so" in Genesis 1:1–2:1.
11. "Nearly 40% of Plant Species Are Very Rare, and Vulnerable to Climate Change," US National Science Foundation, December 6, 2019, https://new.nsf.gov/news/nearly-40-plant-species-are-very-rare-vulnerable.
12. "Facts and Figures," Royal Entomological Society, accessed January 22, 2025, https://www.royensoc.co.uk/understanding-insects/facts-and-figures.
13. Hannah Ritchie, "How Many Species Are There?" *Our World in Data*, November 30, 2022, https://ourworldindata.org/how-many-species-are-there.
14. Genesis 1:31.
15. Psalm 148:1, 3-5.
16. Thomas Lynch, "How We Come to Be the Ones We Are," in Thomas G. Long and Thomas Lynch, *The Good Funeral: Death, Grief, and the Community of Care* (Louisville: Westminster John Knox Press, 2013), 5.
17. For example, Exodus 3:6, 15.
18. Genesis 12:1-3. The biblical figure introduced in Genesis 12 is named Abram; God would later change his name to Abraham.
19. O. Palmer Robertson, *The Christ of the Covenants* (Phillipsburg, NJ: Presbyterian and Reformed Publishing, 1980), 4.

NOTES

20. Lesslie Newbigin, *A Walk through the Bible* (Louisville: Westminster John Knox Press, 1999), 16.
21. Quoted in N. T. Wright, *Simply Christian: Why Christianity Makes Sense* (New York: HarperOne, 2010), 75.
22. Exodus 3:1.
23. Exodus 3:13-14.
24. Robert Alter, *The Hebrew Bible: A Translation with Commentary* (New York: W. W. Norton, 2019), 1:222.
25. Exodus 3:15.
26. Alter, *Hebrew Bible*, 1:222–23.
27. Eugene H. Peterson, *Christ Plays in Ten Thousand Places: A Conversation in Spiritual Theology* (Grand Rapids: Eerdmans, 2005), 157.
28. Genesis 2:7.
29. "Breathing the Name Yahweh," Yahweh's Restoration Ministry, March 28, 2022, https://yrm.org/breathing-the-name-yahweh.
30. Vampire Weekend, "Ya Hey," track 10 on *Modern Vampires of the City*, XL Recordings, 2013.
31. Stephen Prothero, "This, They Believe," *Tampa Bay Times*, May 2, 2010, https://www.tampabay.com/archive/2010/05/02/this-they-believe. Originally published at Stephen Prothero, "Separate Truths," *Boston Globe*, April 25, 2010.
32. John 6:35; 8:12; 10:9, 11, 14; 11:25; 14:6; 15:5.
33. Deuteronomy 6:4, NIV. This text functioned as the core confession of faith for the Jewish people, and Jesus himself quoted it as the very heartbeat of Jewish teaching.
34. For example, John 16:14; 17:4-5.
35. Some in the "classical period" of Christian theology, especially John of Damascus, emphasized the analogy of perichoresis (from which we get the English word *choreography*), or dance, to describe the rhythm of love that exists in the triune relations of God. See Charles C. Twombly, Perichoresis *and Personhood: God, Christ, and Salvation in John of Damascus* (Eugene, OR: Pickwick Publications, 2015).
36. Gregory of Nazianzus, Oration #33, New Advent, accessed March 23, 2025, https://www.newadvent.org/fathers/310233.htm.
37. Hilary of Poitiers, *On the Trinity*, bk. 2, chap. 5, in John R. Willis, ed., *The Teachings of the Church Fathers* (San Francisco: Ignatius Press, 2002), 165.
38. Ian Ker, ed., *The Everyman Chesterton* (New York: Everyman's Library, 2011), 381–82.
39. Julian of Norwich, *Revelations of Divine Love*, trans. Barry Windeatt (Oxford: Oxford University Press, 2015), 164.

CHAPTER FOUR | MISERABLE OFFENDERS

1. G. K. Chesterton, *Orthodoxy* (New York: Dodd, Mead, 1927), 24.
2. *Fleabag*, season 1, episode 6, written by Phoebe Waller-Bridge, directed by Harry Bradbeer, aired September 16, 2016, on BBC Three.
3. *The Simpsons*, season 20, episode 13, "Gone Maggie Gone," written by Matt Groening, James L. Brooks, and Sam Simon, directed by Mike B. Anderson and Chris Clements, aired March 15, 2009, on Fox.
4. You can find two versions of the Ten Commandments in Jewish and Christian Bibles—one in Exodus 20:1-17 and one in Deuteronomy 5:1-21.
5. Robert Alter, *The Hebrew Bible: A Translation with Commentary* (New York: W. W. Norton, 2019), 1:295.
6. Thomas Cahill, *The Gifts of the Jews: How a Tribe of Desert Nomads Changed the Way Everyone Thinks and Feels* (New York: Nan A. Talese/Anchor Books, 1999), 139.
7. Exodus 34:28; Cahill, *Gifts of the Jews*.
8. Exodus 20:1-4, 7.
9. Online Etymology Dictionary, s.v. "worship (*n.*)," accessed January 21, 2025, https://www.etymonline.com/search?q=worship; *Merriam-Webster*, s.v. "worth (*n.*)," accessed January 21, 2025, https://www.merriam-webster.com/dictionary/worth; *Merriam-Webster*, s.v. "ship (*n.*)," accessed January 21, 2025, https://www.merriam-webster.com/dictionary/ship.
10. Martin Luther, *Treatise on Good Works* (1520), sec. 10, accessed January 21, 2025, https://ccel.org/ccel/luther/good_works/good_works.v.html. "Now you see for yourself that all those who do not at all times trust God and do not in all their works or sufferings, life and death, trust in His favor, grace and goodwill, but seek His favor in other things or in themselves, do not keep this Commandment, and practice real idolatry, even if they were to do the works of all the other Commandments, and in addition had all the prayers, fasting, obedience, patience, chastity, and innocence of all the saints combined."
11. N. T. Wright, *Surprised by Scripture: Engaging Contemporary Issues* (New York: HarperOne, 2015), 151–52.
12. Psalm 115:5-9.
13. Genesis 3:17.
14. Romans 8:20-23.
15. John Milton, *Paradise Lost*, book 9, lines 780–84, in *The Complete English Poems*, ed. Gordon Campbell (London: Everyman's Library, 1990), 354.
16. Cornelius Plantinga Jr., *Not the Way It's Supposed to Be: A Breviary of Sin* (Grand Rapids: Eerdmans, 1996), 3.
17. Augustus Toplady, "Rock of Ages," 1776.
18. I'm indebted to Fleming Rutledge for the insights on sin as both guilt

NOTES

and power in this section, particularly in her book *The Crucifixion: Understanding the Death of Jesus Christ* (Grand Rapids: Eerdmans, 2015), 181.
19. The Order for Daily Morning Prayer, *The Book of Common Prayer* (1928), http://justus.anglican.org/resources/bcp/1928/MP.htm.
20. Marilynne Robinson, *Gilead* (New York: Farrar, Straus and Giroux, 2004), 122.
21. Jonathan Haidt, *The Righteous Mind: Why Good People Are Divided by Politics and Religion* (New York: Vintage Books, 2013), xix–xx.
22. Sufjan Stevens, "John Wayne Gacy, Jr.," track 4 on *Illinois*, Asthmatic Kitty Records, 2005.
23. Isaac Watts, "Joy to the World," 1719.
24. W. H. Auden, "September 1, 1939," in *Another Time*, 90th anniv. ed. (London: Faber & Faber, 2019), 105.

CHAPTER FIVE | GOD INCARNO
1. Reza Aslan, interview by John Oliver, *The Daily Show*, season 18, episode 127, aired July 17, 2013, on Comedy Central.
2. Jaroslav Pelikan, *Jesus through the Centuries: His Place in the History of Culture* (New Haven, CT: Yale University Press, 1999), 1.
3. N. T. Wright, *Simply Jesus: A New Vision of Who He Was, What He Did, and Why He Matters* (New York: HarperOne, 2018), 9.
4. Wright, *Simply Jesus*, 9.
5. N. T. Wright, "The Book and the Story," *The Bible in TransMission*, Summer 1997, https://missionworldview.com/wp-content/uploads/2020/06/ea8a85_bd37f8c145d44e99a7aeca44ddb05110.pdf.
6. For a more detailed exploration of the following literary motifs in the Hebrew Scriptures, and more of them not explored here, see Alec Motyer, *Look to the Rock: An Old Testament Background to Our Understanding of Christ*; Lesslie Newbigin, *A Walk through the Bible*; and N. T. Wright, *Jesus and the Victory of God*, *The Challenge of Jesus: Rediscovering Who Jesus Was and Is*, and *Simply Christian: Why Christianity Makes Sense*.
7. N. T. Wright, *The Challenge of Jesus: Rediscovering Who Jesus Was and Is* (Downers Grove, IL: InterVarsity Press, 1999), 62–67.
8. See 2 Samuel 7.
9. Genesis 3:15.
10. Isaiah 65:17, 25.
11. Bruce Willis as Malcolm Crowe and Haley Joel Osment as Cole Sear in *The Sixth Sense*, directed by M. Night Shyamalan (Buena Vista Home Entertainment, 2000), VHS.
12. Matthew 1:22-23.

13. St. Cyril of Alexandria, *On the Unity of Christ*, trans. John Anthony McGuckin (Crestwood, NY: St Vladimir's Seminary Press, 1995), 61.
14. *Bono: In Conversation with Michka Assayas* (New York: Riverhead Books, 2006), 139.
15. Hebrews 4:15.
16. John Calvin, *The Institutes of the Christian Religion*, trans. Henry Beveridge (1845), bk. 2, chap. 8, https://www.ccel.org/ccel/calvin/institutes.v.ix.html.
17. John R. W. Stott, *The Cross of Christ*, 20th anniv. ed. (Downers Grove, IL: IVP Books, 2006), 326–27. In the final sentence, Stott is quoting P. T. Forsyth, *The Justification of God: Lectures for War-Time on a Christian Theodicy*.

CHAPTER SIX | A CRUCIFIX IN A BAR

1. *It's Always Sunny in Philadelphia*, season 7, episode 4, "Sweet Dee Gets Audited," written by Rob McElhenney, Glenn Howerton, and Charlie Day, directed by Matt Shakman, aired October 6, 2011, on FX.
2. Tom Holland, *Dominion: How the Christian Revolution Remade the World* (New York: Basic Books, 2021), 6.
3. Martin Kähler, quoted in Mark Allan Powell, *Introducing the New Testament: A Historical, Literary, and Theological Survey* (Grand Rapids: Baker Academic, 2009), 134. "The passion" is a shorthand way that Christians refer to the events of Jesus' betrayal, suffering, and death.
4. Rowan Williams, *The Sign and the Sacrifice: The Meaning of the Cross and Resurrection* (Louisville: Westminster John Knox Press, 2017), 5–6.
5. Ross Douthat, "Return of the Jesus Wars," *New York Times*, August 3, 2013, https://www.nytimes.com/2013/08/04/opinion/sunday/douthat-return-of-the-jesus-wars.html.
6. 1 Corinthians 15:3.
7. Luke 9:22.
8. Luke 9:44.
9. Luke 18:31-33.
10. The Nicene Creed.
11. The theologian Leanne Van Dyk, a former teacher of mine, points out that the various atonement theories in Christian theology all depict in part the work of God at the Cross of Christ: "There was some kind of victory that took place, some kind of power shift in the universe, some kind of ransom paid, some kind of healing initiated, some ultimate kind of love displayed, some kind of dramatic rescue effected." Quoted in Fleming Rutledge, *The Crucifixion: Understanding the Death of Jesus Christ* (Grand Rapids: Eerdmans, 2017), 210.
12. The most helpful contemporary book on the Atonement, in my opinion,

is Fleming Rutledge's *The Crucifixion*. This section draws on her thorough and substantive work.
13. Eugene H. Peterson, *Christ Plays in Ten Thousand Places: A Conversation in Spiritual Theology* (Grand Rapids: Eerdmans, 2005), 172.
14. Luke 9:31.
15. Williams, *The Sign and the Sacrifice*, 42–43.
16. Colossians 2:13-15.
17. Matthew 27:11, 29, 37.
18. For example, Revelation 5:1-14.
19. Hebrews 10:20.
20. See Rutledge, *Crucifixion*, 462–535.
21. Desmond Tutu, "Statement by Archbishop Desmond Tutu on His Appointment to the Truth and Reconciliation Commission," Department of Justice and Constitutional Development, November 30, 1995, https://www.justice.gov.za/trc/media/pr/1995/p951130a.htm.
22. The insights on the Gospel of John and the literary rhythm of "And the Word became flesh . . . and we have seen his glory" here are drawn from the chapter on John in N. T. Wright, *Following Jesus: Biblical Reflections on Discipleship* (Grand Rapids: Eerdmans, 1995), 34–43.
23. John 1:14. "The Word" is one of the ways John refers to the invisible God who comes to us in Jesus.
24. John 2:11.
25. George Herbert, "The Agony," quoted at Victoria Emily Jones, "The Crushed Christ: An Illustrated Analysis of Herbert's 'The Agony' and Bryant's 'Blood of the Vine,'" *Art & Theology* (blog), March 18, 2018, https://artandtheology.org/2018/03/18/the-crushed-christ-an-illustrated-analysis-of-herberts-the-agony-and-bryants-blood-of-the-vine.

CHAPTER SEVEN | NOTHING TO BE FRIGHTENED OF
1. Julian Barnes, *Nothing to Be Frightened Of* (New York: Vintage Books, 2009), 3.
2. Barnes, *Nothing to Be Frightened Of*, 7.
3. Barnes, *Nothing to Be Frightened Of*, 54.
4. Barnes, *Nothing to Be Frightened Of*, 99.
5. Mark 16:6, KJV.
6. C. S. Lewis, *Surprised by Joy: The Shape of My Early Life* (San Francisco: HarperOne, 2017), 254. "He made short work of what I have called my 'chronological snobbery,' the uncritical acceptance of the intellectual climate common to our own age and the assumption that whatever has gone out of date is on that account discredited."
7. 1 Corinthians 15:3-4.

8. 1 Corinthians 15:14.
9. 1 Corinthians 15:17-19.
10. N. T. Wright, *Simply Christian: Why Christianity Makes Sense* (New York: HarperOne, 2010), 112.
11. John Updike, "Seven Stanzas at Easter," in *Selected Poems*, ed. Christopher Carduff (New York: Alfred A. Knopf, 2018), 15.
12. 1 Corinthians 15:5-7.
13. Quoted in Timothy Keller, *The Reason for God: Belief in an Age of Skepticism* (New York: Penguin Books, 2018), 218.
14. If you'd like to explore this more, the best place to start would be Richard Bauckham, *Jesus and the Eyewitnesses: The Gospels as Eyewitness Testimony* (Grand Rapids: Eerdmans, 2006).
15. N. T. Wright, *The Resurrection of the Son of God*, Christian Origins and the Question of God, vol. 3 (Minneapolis: Fortress Press, 2003), 607–8.
16. You can find a helpful summary of these theories, and the problems with them, in N. T. Wright, *Surprised by Hope: Rethinking Heaven, the Resurrection, and the Mission of the Church* (New York: HarperOne, 2018), 58–63.
17. Wright, *Simply Christian*, 113.
18. Rowan Williams, *Tokens of Trust: An Introduction to Christian Belief* (Louisville: Westminster John Knox Press, 2010), 95.
19. Romans 6:3-4.
20. Ephesians 1:20-21.
21. The Paschal troparion, circa second century.
22. 1 Corinthians 15:26.
23. John Donne, "Holy Sonnets: Death, Be Not Proud," Poetry Foundation, accessed March 27, 2025, https://www.poetryfoundation.org/poems/44107/holy-sonnets-death-be-not-proud.

CHAPTER EIGHT | I'LL BE THERE IN SPIRIT

1. *Midnight in Paris*, directed by Woody Allen (Culver City, CA: Sony Pictures Classics, 2011).
2. John 14:16-18.
3. John 16:7.
4. Charles Taylor, *A Secular Age* (Cambridge, MA: Belknap Press of Harvard University Press, 2007), 539–93.
5. Sam Harris, "There Is No God (and You Know It)," Sam Harris, October 6, 2005, https://www.samharris.org/blog/there-is-no-god-and-you-know-it.
6. Tertullian, quoted at Patrick Toner, "Infallibility," *The Catholic Encyclopedia*, vol. 7 (New York: Robert Appleton, 1910), https://www.newadvent.org/cathen/07790a.htm.

7. Augustine of Hippo, *A Treatise on the Spirit and the Letter*, "Why the Holy Ghost Is Called the Finger of God," accessed January 21, 2025, https://catholiclibrary.org/library/view?docId=/Synchronized-EN/Augustine.SpiritLetter.en.html&chunk.id=00000035.
8. Acts 2:2-4. You can read the whole story in Acts 2:1-42.
9. John 14:23.
10. Acts 2:11.
11. Ephesians 1:14, MSG.
12. 1 Corinthians 15:28.
13. You can read their whole conversation in John 3:1-21.
14. John 3:8.

CHAPTER NINE | SHE'S A HARLOT, SHE'S MY MOTHER

1. Ephesians 4:12.
2. The Apostles' Creed—the earliest summary statement of Christian belief.
3. Robert Waldinger and Marc Schulz, "What the Longest Study on Human Happiness Found Is the Key to a Good Life," *Atlantic*, January 19, 2023, https://www.theatlantic.com/ideas/archive/2023/01/harvard-happiness-study-relationships/672753.
4. Ephesians 2:15.
5. Lesslie Newbigin, *The Gospel in a Pluralist Society* (Grand Rapids: Eerdmans, 1989), 82–83.
6. Miroslav Volf, *Exclusion and Embrace: A Theological Exploration of Identity, Otherness, and Reconciliation*, rev. ed. (Nashville: Abingdon Press, 2019), introduction.
7. Ephesians 2:14.
8. John L'Heureux, "The Long Black Line," *New Yorker*, May 14, 2018, https://www.newyorker.com/magazine/2018/05/21/the-long-black-line.
9. Eugene H. Peterson, *Working the Angles: The Shape of Pastoral Integrity* (Grand Rapids: Eerdmans, 1993), 2.
10. 1 Corinthians 5:1.
11. Dorothy Day, "In Peace Is My Bitterness Most Bitter," Catholic Worker Movement, originally published in *The Catholic Worker*, January 1, 1967, https://catholicworker.org/250-2. Emphasis added.
12. Matthew 11:28-29.
13. Several of those first followers became the authors of the New Testament. So even our holy book is an extension of the testimony of Jesus' community.
14. John 20:21.
15. Teresa of Avila, "Christ Has No Body," Journey with Jesus, accessed May 14, 2025, https://www.journeywithjesus.net/poemsandprayers/3637-Teresa_Of_Avila_Christ_Has_No_Body.

16. Lesslie Newbigin, *The Household of God: Lectures on the Nature of Church* (Eugene, OR: Wipf and Stock, 2008), 27.
17. "Order for the Sacrament of Baptism," Reformed Church in America, accessed March 29, 2025, https://www.rca.org/liturgy/order-for-the-sacrament-of-baptism; also see *Worship the Lord: The Liturgy of the Reformed Church in America* (New York: Reformed Church Press, 2024), 63.

CHAPTER TEN | DURABLE WELFARE

1. Sam Harris, "God-Drunk Society," *Atlantic*, November 2007, https://www.theatlantic.com/magazine/archive/2007/11/god-drunk-society/306303.
2. Why this is the case is a story for another day; if you're interested in how and why this phenomenon developed, I'd encourage you to check out my friend Sara's book: Sara Billups, *Orphaned Believers: How a Generation of Christian Exiles Can Find the Way Home* (Grand Rapids: Baker Books, 2023).
3. See, for example, Matthew 24:36-44.
4. The Nicene Creed.
5. N. T. Wright, *Surprised by Hope: Rethinking Heaven, the Resurrection, and the Mission of the Church* (New York: HarperOne, 2018), 149.
6. Wright, *Surprised by Hope*, 93.
7. Revelation 21:1-4.
8. Isaiah 2:2-4.
9. Isaiah 65:17-18, 25.
10. 1 Corinthians 15:20, 28.
11. The Apostles' Creed.
12. Psalm 98:7-9.
13. Miroslav Volf, *Exclusion and Embrace: A Theological Exploration of Identity, Otherness, and Reconciliation*, rev. ed. (Nashville: Abingdon Press, 2019), 299–300.
14. Cormac McCarthy, *No Country for Old Men* (New York: Alfred A. Knopf, 2005), 159.
15. Isaiah 2:5.
16. 1 Corinthians 15:58.